Hugh Lasgarn grew up in a small Welsh
village and trained at Glasgow Veterinary
College. Since graduating, he has lived and
worked in the Welsh Border country that he
loves and where he met and married his wife.
His first book, *Vet in Green Pastures* was an
instant success on its publication in 1985, and
it was followed by a second, equally popular
volume *Vet for All Seasons*.

*Hugh Lasgarn*

# VET IN
# A STORM

FONTANA/Collins

First issued by Souvenir Press Ltd, 1987
First issued in Fontana Paperbacks 1988

Copyright © 1987 by Hugh Lasgarn

Printed and bound in Great Britain by
William Collins Sons & Co. Ltd, Glasgow

*To Sara and Joanna*

There are ships to sail the oceans
And aeroplanes to fly
But Whoever made the seagull
Was a Very Clever Guy.

Hugh Lasgarn
April 1987

# 1

'It's the little things that get to you, in practice,' said Bob Hacker, when I joined him in Ledingford.

How right he was – a little boy and a bird.

Had Warrior, Paxton's champion bull, died during the operation, I would have suffered the wrath of an infuriating old man – but his bull survived. Far more crushing was the look in Billy Bent's eyes when I told him Peter was dead.

Paxton was a belligerent, self-made North Country bachelor who bred magnificent pedigree Herefords, and Billy Bent was just a little boy with a budgerigar – called Peter.

But, as Bob said, 'It's the little things . . .!'

It all started when Billy's budgie died: a little blue budgie that he brought to the surgery in St Mark's Square, just a few weeks after I came to Ledingford.

Billy was about eight years old at the time, a slightly built, shy little fellow, shabbily dressed in a threadbare pullover, patched trousers and uncomfortable, oversize boots. Yet if Billy looked a pathetic picture standing there, cage in hand, in the consulting room, his budgie, Peter, looked even worse.

Peter was suffering from impaction of the crop caused by insufficient grit in the diet, a common complication with such a deficiency. Liquid paraffin had not worked and the only alternative measure was an operation to relieve the pressure. Just a small incision would be needed and, as I could foresee no obvious complications, I assured Billy his pet would be all right.

1

My carefree optimism was bolstered by the fact that, having that morning operated successfully upon Paxton's valuable pedigree Hereford bull, my spirits were riding high and my confidence was enhanced.

The occasion had put my reputation firmly on the line. Removing the corns from between the massive bull's hind toes had necessitated a general anaesthetic – an extremely precarious procedure in a bull of such size. Despite the fact that McBean, one of the partners in the practice, had not arrived in time to help me, it had been a success. Such was my elation at the achievement that sedating a budgerigar held no terrors.

But Peter died under the ether – even before I had attempted to correct the condition. And I had to tell Billy – little Billy Bent, whose last words to his pet were: 'I'll be back for you Pete – now, don' you worry.'

He did not cry when I told him. I remember thinking it would have been easier for me if he had. He just kept searching my face with his sad little eyes, as if I had spoken in a foreign language that he did not understand.

Of all the many and varied experiences I encountered in my early days in practice, it was that very simple one, of having to tell a small boy his budgie had died, that devastated me the most.

I mentioned the incident to Paxton on my next visit to see Warrior and, to my surprise, he invited the boy to his Donhill estate where, among his superb livestock, he possessed a fabulous collection of exotic birds.

'Bring him to me and he shall have the smartest pair of budgerigars in the county to go home with!'

Diana, my girlfriend, was invited as well and, one summer's afternoon, the three of us drove out to his home.

Paxton acted like a benevolent uncle, a transformation I found incredible.

It was a gloriously hot day; a strawberry tea was served on the lawn and Billy, though initially finding the laden table overwhelming, soon tucked in with enthusiasm. Afterwards we were given a conducted tour and saw Warrior, the herd of pedigree Herefords; the thoroughbred Arabs, the perfect flock of Suffolks, the rose gardens and the lake. Finally we came to the aviary.

The little lad was lost for words, as if he could not absorb the colour and intensity of sound that enveloped him, but once he settled down he could hardly contain himself.

Finally the old man, true to his word, produced a pair of budgerigars in a brand-new cage: one green and one blue, like Peter.

It was touching, but the most poignant moment was to come.

Billy had gone ahead, to climb the paddock rails and give a last wave to the Herefords.

'Well, young man! Have you enjoyed yourself?' asked Paxton, beaming expansively.

'Yes, please! Thank you very much!' said the boy, in a rush of enthusiasm.

'I suppose one day, you'd like to be a farmer like me, with all these cows?' Paxton continued, grandly.

Billy gazed about, his eyes trailing from the grazing herd across the lake to the lawns, the big house and back again.

Then he took hold of Diana's hand, looked up into the old man's face and said:

'No, thank you very much. I'd rather be like Mr Lasgarn!'

I often wondered afterwards how things might have turned out if he had said 'Yes!' to that wealthy old man.

In a story with a happy ending, Paxton would have taken the little orphan under his wing, given him an education, given him attention, perhaps even given him a home – but Paxton never mentioned him again.

There was a point when I thought the old man might have a change of heart. It was when he had suffered a major emotional upset – his aviary had been ravaged in an act of spite and his beautiful exotic birds massacred. When Billy heard, he offered to return the budgerigars he had been given. The old man seemed moved by the gesture at the time, but never took it up.

For my part, I encouraged Billy's interest in his tiny flock and helped him build a small aviary in the back yard of the terraced house where he lived with his Gran.

The birds bred and Billy became quite knowledgeable about their habits. Often he would call at the end of evening surgery, on the pretence of asking for some advice, though he knew if he timed it right I would give him a lift home and stop for a few minutes to see how his enterprise was developing.

★ ★ ★

The first time I suspected Billy was unwell was on an evening when I had finished rather earlier than usual.

I was just turning out of the yard into East Street when, in the mirror, I saw him running along the pavement after me.

Pulling up, I wound down my window and sat waiting for him to catch up – but he did not do so and when I looked back I saw, to my horror, his frail little figure slumped against the wall.

I was out of the car and to him in a second.

'Billy, what's the matter?'

He was wheezing and gasping pitifully, his face ashen, and he gripped my sleeve tightly.

Gradually he calmed and I walked him slowly to the car.

'I was late,' he said, still breathing heavily. 'I had to go ... I had ... had to go to the shops for Gran.'

'I was early finishing,' I explained. 'Now just you sit quietly and get your breath.'

He seemed to recover fairly quickly after that, but did not say much as we drove along to Farrs Court.

'Do you get out of breath much?' I asked him.

He nodded. 'Only sometimes.'

'Has Gran taken you to the doctor?'

He shook his head. 'She gives me stuff to sniff up –

"Flying Boston". She puts the towel over me head and it makes me eyes run!'

'Friar's Balsam', I said. He nodded again.

When we got to his place, while he went on into the garden, I searched out Gran and told her about the incident.

'He's always been "chesty",' she said, 'but I can't get him to the doctor, on no account. What with losing his Mam and Dad, an' all them hospital visits with it, I suppose you can understand.'

She looked at me intently for a few seconds, then pushed some grey strands of thinning hair from her forehead and said, 'Perhaps if you had a word with him, he might.'

In the yard, Billy had just caught up a blue budgie and was holding it ready for me to see.

'His beak is growing curly,' he said. 'He's got all the things to rough it off, but he won't use them.'

I took the bird from him and examined it.

'I'll bring the clippers next time and trim it up.'

'Will you show me how to do it?' he asked.

'Of course I will, Billy.'

'An' will you do something else for me? Somethin' special?'

'What's that?'

He held the little blue budgie closer to him and said: 'Will you help me to be a bird vet when I grow up?'

'Well, you can't just be a bird vet, not to start with anyway,' I said, trying not to make it sound unlikely. 'You'd have to study about all the animals, first.'

'I'm not clever enough to do 'em all,' he said, with disarming honesty. 'I'd just like to learn about birds. Will you help me?'

I could see my opportunity and grasped it.

'Well, if you want to be a vet, even a bird vet, you've got to be fit and well. No good trying to help sick birds if you're not well yourself, is it?' He turned away, sensing what I was going to say. 'I'll help you, but only if you let Gran

5

take you to Doctor Brown to clear up that bad chest of yours.'

'I don' like doctors,' he said, without looking up.

'They're only like vets, except they look after people instead of animals,' I said.

'People vets!' Billy smiled at last. I nodded. 'People vets!' he repeated. 'That's funny.'

'Will you go, Billy?'

'Yes,' he said, holding the bird at arm's length and studying it intently. 'An' then, when I'm a bird vet,' he told the tiny creature, 'I can do yer beak me'self.'

Practice was very busy and I forgot about the beak trimming, nor did Billy call to remind me.

Then, one lunchtime, I phoned back to surgery from a call box at Lindenchurch to see if there were any more cases in the area, before going home. Miss Billings answered.

'Police Constable Packham called this morning to see if Billy Bent was here. He isn't with you, is he?'

I had taken him on calls occasionally, but only at weekends or when he was off school, and her news disturbed me.

'He's been missing since early morning,' she said. 'Can't find him anywhere.'

'Where on earth can he be?' I asked, my mind already exploring the possibilities.

'They really don't seem to know; they've looked everywhere. PC Packham said he was off down to the river, from here,' she added. 'I do hope the little mite's all right.'

Going down to the river – that was a terrible thought. Surely Billy was too sensible to take any risks and too young to contemplate anything more sinister – and why should he, anyway? It was an excessively macabre thought and I dismissed it. 'I'll go to Farrs Court now,' I said anxiously. 'See if there's anything I can do.'

For a few seconds after replacing the receiver, I stood in the box and tried to reason why Billy should want to run away, if that was what had happened – at least, in one way, I hoped that was what had happened.

On arriving, I let myself into the passageway of the little terraced house and found Gran in the kitchen, staring at the fire in the iron grate. She turned round as I entered.

'Oh! Mr Lasgarn!' she said, getting up, her eyes wet with tears. 'Where is he?'

'I don't know, Gran,' I said, putting my arm round her shoulder and sitting her gently down again. 'But don't worry, we'll find him wherever he is.' She shook her head and covered her eyes with her wrinkled hands. 'Did he say anything at all, before he went?' I asked.

'I didn't see him,' she explained. 'When I got up this morning, he wasn't there; but last night he was worried about his birds.'

'His birds!'

She nodded. 'He took them with him.'

'Took them with him! Why would he do that?'

'It was the doctor, you see. We went, like you said, and he examined him all over. Then, when he had finished, he told me it was a sort of asthma. Then he gave us some medicine, said Billy had to have plenty of fresh air – and he had to get rid of his birds!'

Her last words hit me like a rock! Of course! Asthma! Asthma aggravated by feathers! Not that it was conclusive as a trigger factor, for the condition could be precipitated in so many ways; but Doctor Brown's preventative measures were logical and acceptable – acceptable that was, to a comprehending adult. But to a small boy orphaned at eight, whose birds were possibly his sole reason for living, there was no rationale.

Would he have gone to my house – to see Diana, now my wife? He might have done, but then she would have rung – but who would she ring? Gran did not have a phone.

I drove home full of hope, but he was not there. Diana had been in all morning and nobody had called.

7

I could not eat lunch, but she insisted I had a cup of coffee. Together we went through the possibilities.

'He wouldn't harm those birds,' I said. 'I know he wouldn't. He's taking them somewhere where they'll be safe. Some place he knows . . .'

'And someone he can trust,' said Diana.

She looked across the table at me – and we thought of it together:

'PAXTON! HE'S GONE TO PAXTON!'

I stumbled to the phone. It took ages to get through; then Paxton himself answered:

'Billy who?' barked the old man.

'Billy Bent.' I repeated. 'The little boy with the budgerigars – remember? You gave him a pair and he offered to give you them back, that time.'

'No!' said Paxton 'Why?'

I explained that Billy had gone missing and taken his birds.

'Why should he come here?'

'It was just a thought,' I said, annoyed at his unsympathetic response. 'He must be looking for a safe place for his birds and I think he trusted you.'

There was silence. I waited a few seconds.

'Mr Paxton?'

I heard him clear his throat. 'No. He hasn't been here,' he said, but his tone had mellowed slightly . . . 'No,' he repeated, 'he hasn't been here.'

'Heartless old bastard,' I fumed, as I put down the phone.

'Hugh!' reprimanded Diana. 'Anyway, how could he get to Donhill, it's miles away?'

'He'd walk. He might not be very strong, but he's a determined little blighter.'

'Well, if he's walking, he surely won't be there yet,' she concluded. 'He'll still be on the way.'

She was right. It was a good twelve miles to Paxton's, and even if he had set out at dawn he would not go very fast, especially if he was carrying his pets.

I drove abnormally slowly, for my usual pace was considerably faster; but I wanted to make sure Billy was not resting in any of the field gateways or up the small by-roads. When I got to Easthope village, I stopped to make some enquiries – but drew a blank. So on I pressed to Donhill.

Whatever the season, Donhill looks impressive, sitting as it does on a high point at the end of the valley. The magnificent house, the barns and stockyards, set off by the highly painted rails that line, with perfect continuity, the tarmac driveway that runs from the road.

I drove up slowly, despondent that I had not found him. At the end of the first paddock, the cattle had collected near the fence, just where a well grown beech hedge separated it from the home fields. Something had obviously attracted their attention, for they were unsettled and inquisitive, poking their heads over the rails and looking about.

I got out of the car to make a closer inspection, but could see no obvious cause for their behaviour until I glanced around the hedge cover and looked on up the drive towards the buildings.

There was Billy, socks down, pullover crumpled, making his way towards Donhill – a shoebox tucked beneath each arm.

I was about to call out with relief, when I caught sight of a figure at the gate.

A tall figure, dressed in a navy-blue pinstriped suit with a rose in the lapel, and tapping a silver-topped cane on the ground, while he watched the little fellow approach. It was Paxton waiting for Billy.

I stood and watched in silence as he drew near to the old man. He did not run or even quicken his pace, nor did Paxton move towards him.

There was no way I could hear what was said: nor did I need to, for the earnestness of Billy's movements and the gentle nodding of old Paxton's head said it all.

They stood together for a few minutes, then Paxton put

hand on Billy's shoulder and, turning his back on me, hepherded the little figure towards the house.

I sat in the car for nearly fifteen minutes. I should really have gone straight up and rung home to say he had been found and was safe, but I felt it was a time to let things gently settle, a time to let innocent youth and belligerent old age warm together. So I sat and watched the Herefords grazing on the summer grass.

When, finally, I did go up to the house, the housekeeper showed me into Paxton's great study, a place that often reminded me of pictures I had seen of the Oval Office at the White House.

Paxton was seated in his great leather chair and opposite him sat Billy, eating ham sandwiches; a half-full glass of milk on the desk before him.

When I entered he looked rather startled:

'Mr Paxton's 'aving me birds!' he blurted. 'Aren't you, Mr Paxton?'

Paxton nodded. 'They'll be safe with me, Billy,' he said.

'Good job you're safe, too, Billy,' I added. 'Gran's been ever so worried.'

'They were goin' to take them away,' he said. 'That doctor, what you sent me to.'

'I was only thinking of your chest, Billy.'

'I don't care about me chest, I'd rather have me birds, an' you said I could be a bird vet, if I went. An' how can I be a bird vet if they takes me birds?'

He picked up the glass in front of him and buried his nose in it.

Paxton looked directly at me and a wicked smile crossed his face – not malicious, just mischievous, making him seem quite genial. Then he got his arrow in:

'Well, Mr Lasgarn, you're a professional. Answer that one!'

He never let go, did Paxton. He had not forgotten our altercation when I had appeared somewhat reluctant about operating on his bull, Warrior. I had merely been trying to point out the risks, when he had laid into me:

10

'Risks!' he had roared down the phone. 'You're a professional – you're trained to take risks!'

So his goading about Billy's question had a cutting edge: he never let anyone off the hook!

I had been surprised how well Billy's chest had stood up to the marathon from Ledingford, but as is sometimes apparent in asthmatics, excitement or nervous tension can be more provocative than physical exertion. I could see Billy was beginning to wheeze and so could Paxton.

He stood up and looked out of the window behind his desk to a vista that took in the lawns, rose gardens and lake, before rolling away towards the Malvern Hills.

'What about fish?' he said. 'Ever thought of fish, Billy?'

Billy appeared a trifle bemused and put the now empty glass carefully back on the desk.

'Ain't got no pond, like you,' he said. 'So I couldn't have no fish.'

Paxton turned to face him.

'Now that my lad, is where you're wrong,' he said. 'Have you finished your sandwiches?'

'Yes. Please. Thank you very much,' said Billy.

'You come along with me. You don't need a pond. Lasgarn!' he tried to glower but it did not quite come off and I knew why: he was enjoying himself too much. 'Lasgarn! You come along, too. See my new enterprise.'

Once again he put his hand on little Billy's shoulder, guiding him gently to the door. We went through the hall, down a long passage and then turned into an alcove that ended in a spiral staircase, leading to the cellars.

I followed behind until we came to a green baize door. It was a double door, the baize part pulling outwards, the inner, wooden part going inwards.

Paxton spread out his arms to allow Billy to walk through before him; then he followed and I came behind.

The room was low and softly lit; peaceful and relaxing, devoid of any noise, save for a background of muffled 'blurps'. It was a cavern full of colour and gentle rhythmic motion – a vast series of aquaria full of unbelievable swimming creatures. Not just freshwater or tropical fish, but creatures of the deep: squids, octopus, anemones; a marine wonderland there in the heart of Herefordshire.

If Billy was amazed, his reaction was no greater than mine. I had never seen anything to equal it. There must have been twelve or more tanks around the walls, all beautifully lit and crystal-clear, each one a cameo of life beneath the waves – it was breathtaking.

Paxton always revelled in producing a sensation of awe in the spectators to his achievements, but in this case I was fully willing to bow to his creation.

But then, I knew him and understood what motivated his desire for perfection; as for Billy, he just stood in the middle of the room, put his hands to his cheeks and stared.

'Are these all fish?' he asked, without taking his eyes off the tanks.

'Some are and some aren't,' said Paxton. 'Beautiful, don't you think?'

And indeed they were. I had never seen such colour and melody of movement.

Billy went forward to one of the largest tanks, putting his face quite close to the glass. There were corals and shells and transparent waving things, to which I could not put a name; all blending in a mix of psychedelic beauty.

He stood for some time, mesmerised, his hands still on his reddened cheeks. Then suddenly he turned to face us.

'Could I be a fish vet?' he said.

'A fish vet, Billy . . . ?'

'Of course he can be a fish vet!' barked Paxton, in his old aggressive style. 'If you want to be a fish vet, you can be one, my boy. I'll see to that!'

'I'd like to do that,' said Billy. 'It could be as good as a bird vet, couldn't it?'

'Of course it could,' said Paxton, 'Eh, Lasgarn?'

The old man and the boy stood gazing at the tanks, both linked by a common desire: to feel a sense of fulfilment, a sense of purpose; and, as I watched from the shadows, I knew they had both found it. For there in front of me was

12

Paxton, sharing what he had struggled all his life for, yet found wanting – and Billy, who was only small and a bit wheezy, but in spite of that was to become, in time, one of the country's leading marine biologists.

And as for me, I was learning that what I had once been told by a crusty old Scots vet, when I went before the Army Board for my deferment, was true – though at the time I thought his statement cynical.

I can picture him now, sitting on the right of the resplendent army major who was chairing the board and peering over the tops of his National Health specs.

'Lasgarn,' he had said, when his turn came to make an observation, 'just remember this. There's more in life than calving cows.'

I thought he was a miserable old fart at the time – but there was a lot in what he said.

# 2

It was a few weeks later that I was awakened from my sleep by the telephone bell – only to find myself entangled in an utterly mystifying conversation.

Night-time telephone calls were invariably emergencies, the degree of urgency evoking an element of panic in the coolest of clients. As a result, the facts of the situation were not always readily or correctly ascertained – especially as, like many of my colleagues, I was often not instantly receptive at such an hour.

'Is that the vet? Come quickly – Bodger is in a terrible state!' – such a message could be fraught with problems if Bodger's whereabouts did not immediately come to mind and his owner rang off before supplying details. Often the words were garbled, the pitch of the voice altered, accents more pronounced or the whole thing somewhat incoherent as a result of a little 'lubrication', recently imbibed. However, over the years, I had managed to calm, decipher and respond to such clients' requests without mishap.

On this occasion, however, my initial reaction on lifting the phone was to wonder how this earful of chatter fitted into the dream I had been happily enjoying. Then I began to suspect a hoax. They did try it on, though not frequently; the last had dragged me out at midnight to an empty house in Ledingford, together with the Gas Board, Water Board, two taxis and a conjuror, who had been tricked into thinking he was to entertain at a midnight party. However, after listening for some time to the babble and eventually concluding that the voice, though unintelligible, was human, I was taken aback by the sound of a barking dog. Not, as one might expect, in the background, but coming right down the phone – the caller was now doing animal impersonations!

Gradually my ears began to pick out phrases that sounded like 'buddah-taya', 'waga-waga', 'fuja-raja' and 'bwud', punctuated with the interminable dog impressions, they could have been code words, for all I knew, but gave me no clue to what was happening. Even worse, the caller rang off without giving any intimation of his name or address.

I replaced the receiver unsteadily and lay back on my pillow.

'Who was it?' murmured Diana, only momentarily surfacing from her slumbers.

'A ... Chinaman,' I said thoughtfully, enlightenment slowly dawning, 'a Chinaman in distress.'

Diana responded with a drowsy chuckle, turned over onto her side and went back to sleep. For a minute or so, I closed my eyes as well, allowing my dulled senses to organise themselves, only to be jerked into full awareness when she suddenly sat up in bed and said, 'A WHAT!'

'A Chinaman,' I repeated. 'And a lucky thing it was, too!'

'Hugh – are you all right?' She turned and, through half-opened eyes, studied my face intently. 'Why, at one o'clock in the morning, is it lucky for a Chinaman to ring you up?'

'Because he didn't give his name,' I said. 'That's why.'

Diana stared at me in bewilderment, blinked as if to confirm to herself that she was not involved in some dream-time veterinary fantasy, then put her arm round me and said, 'Darling, you're working too hard.'

Her concern was understandable, for the practice had been extremely busy during the winter months. Yet, when I said 'lucky' I really meant it, for it so happened that there was only one oriental gentleman in Ledingford in those days – a Mr Wang who, with his family, ran a laundry and small café down by the cattle market. Had it not been for his distinctive accent, I would have been unable to attend

15

the emergency – something the Royal College of Veterinary Surgeons, who enact the code of conduct to which all practitioners are bound, would not have smiled upon too kindly.

After convincing Diana that I was not suffering from delusions or on the verge of a nervous breakdown, I dressed and went down to the car. She had not been entirely convinced of my sanity and had offered to come with me, but I allayed her fears by promising to ring her from the Wangs', when I had attended to the case.

I drove on my uncertain mission through the narrow streets of old Ledingford, the overhanging eves and rooftops giving the ancient buildings the appearance of elderly people, round-shouldered, leaning one upon the other as they snoozed the night away. The slightest of uneasy feelings crossed my mind. Was this a hoax, too? Would I meet up once again with my companions of the night – the Gas man, the Water Board official, the taxi drivers and the poor 'tricked-again' conjuror, outside some empty dwelling?

Then I began to question my assumptions. After all, there were a hell of a lot of Chinese in the world; the fact that one of them had happened to ring me up in the middle of the night, without giving his name and address, and I thought I knew which one it was, could be construed by some as being a trifle overconfident.

But, as I rounded the corner into Whitefriar Street, there was no mistaking my port of call. For assembled upon the pavement outside a double-fronted shop, stood the whole of the Wang family in night attire, with the exception of the proprietor, Mr Wang himself, who, still in his day clothes, was hopping up and down in the middle of the road like an agitated parrot.

Before I could even stop, he ran over to the car and yanked at the door handle. Then, when I attempted to alight, he grabbed the arm of my thick-knit pullover – which was already two sizes too large, but handy for night calls – and pulled upon the shoulder and sleeve, making it

16

even larger. On top of all this, my left foot stuck beneath the clutch pedal as he attempted to tear me from my vehicle, so that I twisted my ankle and shouted at the pain – a reaction that served only to increase his agitation and generate more high-pitched, unintelligible (to me, at least) outpourings.

Mr Wang's frantic behaviour was completely out of character. Although I knew little of him, on the few occasions when I had seen him shuffling about Ledingford or pushing his large wheeled laundry cart, he had epitomised the courteous, slightly deferential yet mysterious aura of his ancient race. He reminded me of a smaller version of Charlie Chan, the intrepid oriental detective whose appearances at the 'flea-pit' – as the Capitol Cinema at Abergranog was known in my youth – I never failed to miss.

The main difference between Wang and Chan was sartorial; for the latter invariably wore a dark suit and sported a black Homburg, whereas Mr Wang, being café proprietor-cum-laundryman, was perhaps somewhat more authentic. He regularly dressed in a sugarbag-blue shirt with a high collar and baggy trousers to match, fronted with a snow-white apron that reached his ankles, giving the appearance of a skirt. His headgear, too, was constant: a small, brimless black hat. Beneath this, his face, creased and yellow, was dominated by piercing dark eyes and his moustache, whilst not as luxuriant as that of Charlie Chan, was equally oriental in style. But the fiend dragging me into the shop and shouting, *Meesa Lhassan! Meesa Lhassan!* was a very different person indeed!

As I was drawn forcibly through the door, the Wang family, of whom there was quite a number, and who, clad as they were, resembled part of the chorus line from *Turandot*, parted almost ceremoniously and for a moment I feared I might be the victim of a sinister plot – especially as Mr Wang continued to screech the words 'buddah-taya' almost hysterically, like some crazed religious fanatic. Then, to my relief, I heard the now familiar 'wag-waga', 'fuja-raja' and 'bwud', followed by three new ones – 'bluv-ver', 'hoy-de' and, to my surprise, 'Cardiff'!

Into the narrow passage we went, amid a mixed aroma of steam and spice as we passed between laundry room and café, Mr Wang, now behind, propelling me onward. When we moved into the light, I noticed his features to be not only tense but of an extraordinary pallor.

Finally, we arrived outside a red door, one of three leading from a small hallway at the end of the passage, where we halted and, for the first time, Mr Wang ceased his interminable chattering.

At this point, I decided to try and get some facts: 'Now, Mr Wang,' I began. 'Calm down and tell me what is going on . . .'

Mr Wang launched into another spasm of agitation from which I gathered nothing, but when I placed my hand upon the knob of the door, he went instantly silent again. And, glancing over my shoulder, I saw a row of round, apprehensive faces of varying size, glued to my every move.

What lay behind the red door? Was Hugh Lasgarn, country vet, about to slay the Chinese Dragon of Ledingford? Would the triumph lead to accolades similar to those awarded to other dragon-slayers, and St Lasgarn's Day become a public holiday? Then I remembered Diana's suggestion that I was working too hard and, dismissing my flight of fancy, opened the door and entered what appeared to be a storeroom.

As if I had thrown a switch, my action set off an outburst of barking – not dissimilar to Mr Wang's effort on the phone – but nowhere near a dragon's roar.

Then my eye fell upon the motivator of the whole affair and the explanation of the situation became clear as the puzzling words fell into place.

There before me stood a small 'buddah-taya' who had seemingly caught his 'waga-waga' in the 'fuja-raja' and there was 'bwud' all over the place. Or, in Herefordian: a Border Terrier had caught his tail in the fridge door that was swinging ajar behind him, and the whole place was a bloody mess!

To complete the translation, it also eventually transpired that the dog belonged to Mr Wang's 'bluvver', who had gone for a short 'hoy-de' to ... Cardiff!

Despite having the mystery unveiled and the extent of the problem revealed, resolving it was not as easy as it looked.

Firstly, the slightest move in the direction of my fiery little patient caused him to back into a corner, raise his volume and bare his teeth, to indicate his extreme displeasure at the whole messy business.

Bleeding appendages, such as tails and ears, are extremely difficult to cope with at the best of times, for their constant wagging or flapping is not conducive to the formation of a clot, and bandaging such extremities is a far from easy procedure. Placing a tourniquet for a short period around the base of the tail or ear is effective, but the little 'buddah-taya' was in no mood to co-operate – and he was making that noisily obvious.

The injured tail-end glowed ominously, like a warning beacon, matching the bright red collar around his neck, and although it appeared to have ceased haemorrhaging, I felt that, for safety's sake, I should take a closer look.

'Have you got a lead?' I shouted to Mr Wang, who was peering round the door, his face still exhibiting the unusual pallor.

'Lee! Lee!' he repeated, frowning. 'Lee! Lee!'

'Dog lead!' I emphasised. 'This ....' Then, putting my head on one side, I pretended to lift my neck with an invisible rope, in the manner of a hanging man.

Mr Wang's face lit up. 'Ah! Lee! Lee!' he shouted, holding up his hands in a mixture of relief and delight at understanding my request. Then he turned to the assembled junior Wangs and burbled some orders that were immediately followed by the scampering of innumerable feet throughout the building. Eventually a hand appeared round the door, from which dangled a lead, a red one, matching the Border Terrier's collar.

'Now, "how to bell the cat"', I said as I folded it in my hands. Mr Wang, who was standing just inside the doorway, looked at me curiously. 'Cat,' he said, slowly, 'no cat.'

I quickly realised that there was enough confusion without adding to it and nodded in agreement, smiling as I did so, in an attempt to indicate I was not serious. But Mr Wang remained somewhat puzzled.

However, 'belling the cat' or 'snaring the dog' – whatever I wished to call it – was not going to be easy. There was no way the lead could be clipped into the collar in correct fashion, so I folded the shank through the handpiece, in the manner of a lasso.

'What's his name?' I asked.

'He caw . . . Chum-Chum!' Mr Wang informed me from behind.

It was a title that little suited my opponent at that particular time – and opponent he was, for every time I advanced, cooing his name, he responded with a distinctly hostile reaction.

After several attempts and 'passes', as the bullfighting term has it, and once getting caught in the corner myself – when he darted by me and the rôles, for a few seconds, were reversed – I decided I was using the wrong tactics; perhaps Mr Wang should try? It was, after all, his brother's dog, and the animal was presumably used to him.

Mr Wang froze like a Ming vase and emitted a moan, characteristic of a dying cow, when I suggested the idea. But I passed the red lead into his sweating palms and urged him to have a go.

He gave a great sigh, then, crouching in the style of a demented spider, pushed out his hands, the lead dangling at their extremity, and advanced, uttering what sounded to me like mystical incantations. But each time he moved forward, the Border Terrier, free from human apprehensions and with a pain in his tail, reacted aggressively with a sharp, explosive vocal response.

'Go on, Mr Wang!' I encouraged. 'Remember Confucius! "A barking dog never bites"!'

Mr Wang turned towards me, the red lead now dancing at the end of his fingers like an electric eel, his eyes reduced to tiny black slits; his colour was now not merely unusual but completely indescribable.

'Meesa Lhassan,' he said breathlessly, 'you know ploverb. I know ploverb.' Then his face turned into an explosive balloon. 'BUT,' he yelled at the top of his voice, '*Does bwuddy dog know ploverb?*'

With that, he threw the red lead high into the air and ran out of the storeroom, leaving me alone with my hostile patient.

The whole affair now seemed completely out of hand, but rescue came in the form of one of the middle-sized, junior Wangs who produced a fine rope net, used in the laundry room for holding small items together, before immersion in the wash boiler. Without any assistance, he cast his net over Chum-Chum with the minimum of fuss and the maximum of efficiency, coupled with no little style. The little Border Terrier struggled for a few moments, then lay perfectly still, succumbing to the restraint.

Once caught, he was no hindrance and I was able to sedate him further with an injection. When the drug had taken effect, I examined the tip of his tail, which had been split horizontally by its compression in the refrigerator door and required two stitches. These I inserted and taped and, as Mr Wang's brother, who actually lived in Worcester, was returning to collect his pet in a few days, I advised, with tongue in cheek, that he took Chum-Chum to a vet there, to have the stitches removed in due course.

Before leaving, I rang Diana. 'I'm not mad and it was a Chinaman,' I told her.

'Don't say he was having trouble with his Pekingese!' she retorted.

'No, a "Buddah-Taya",' I replied.

And in the manner of an excited midnight client, I rang off without imparting any further information.

# 3

Had Chum-Chum not been possessed of such a long 'waga-waga', as Mr Wang had called it, the incident of the fridge door might never have occurred.

Indeed, this argument is used by some who are in favour of the docking of dogs' tails – in that there is less risk of injury and pain through being caught up in brambles, wire and, of course, doors. Others are of the opinion that the operation is a mutilation and an interference with nature. Although I was to modify my views as to the morality of such a procedure during a later period, in my early days in practice I carried it out as and when requested.

Not that I was unaware of the contention over the matter; indeed, I was reminded of the force of persuasion one afternoon, when confronted by an extremely emotional female member of the Kennel Club, a power-fully built Boxer bitch called Mika – who imprinted her opinions on more than just my memory.

I had received a call from a Mr Janis Jolokowski, a Polish gentleman who lived in one of the smarter parts of Leding-ford. He was telephoning from London, where both he and his wife were visiting the business in which he was involved, the importation of fine carpets. At his home, a large Victorian mansion just off the Putsley Road, his Boxer bitch had given birth to six puppies during their absence. Apparently, the youngsters had had a trouble-free arrival into the world and Mika herself was well; but Mr Jolokowski wished the pups to have their tails docked and dew-claws trimmed.

He knew that this was best carried out in the first forty-eight hours following the whelping; but as it appeared that both his wife and himself were going to be detained in the City rather longer than expected, he asked if I could go that afternoon and attend to the matter.

'There is only my mother at the house,' he informed me, in extremely good English. 'She is old and a trifle deaf, but will show you where the puppies are. She only speaks Polish,' he added, 'but if you are able to give me your approximate time of arrival, I will telephone her. Then she will be able to take Mika away. I think it would be safer for you,' he concluded, in a slightly sinister tone.

I told him I would go at three o'clock and he said he would make the necessary arrangements.

The house was very imposing, set in exceptionally well tended grounds and standing back from the road. The long drive ended in a gravelled forecourt, the surfacing of which gave even my little Ford an opulent touch, as the small stones crunched grandly beneath the tyres.

It took several pulls on the bell-knob before there was any response to the succession of jangles that penetrated deep inside the house.

Eventually, a figure materialised behind the coloured, leaded lights of the door and, when bolts had been drawn, old Mrs Jolokowski let me in.

She was small, bent and dressed from head to toe in black, with delicate little lace ruffs at her neck and around the cuffs of her sleeves. Her shoes were black, too, pointed and very shiny.

But it was her expression that was so appealing, for though her hair, tied in a bun, was thick and black and her face wrinkled like old parchment, through the creases peeped the greyest of grey eyes – a Polish Granny, if ever I saw one.

What with Mr Wang and now old Mrs Jolokowski, I was beginning to wonder if I had the nucleus of an international veterinary practice growing up in Ledingford.

She said nothing, but beckoned me to follow. The hall-way was large and oak-panelled, with shiny red tiles

23

covering the floor. Along the length of it was laid a very fine Turkish runner and opening off were several large rooms, each with its door ajar. There was a rather cathedral-like atmosphere about the place and I found myself sniffing the air for incense.

The old lady first led me into a dining-room, furnished in Jacobean style – the centrepiece being a massive table covered with a white sheet. She straightened one corner and looked up at me for approval.

For a moment I was puzzled; then I realised that the vast shrouded surface was my operating table! When you have space, use it, I was taught, but it was a little superfluous to requirements.

I nodded and she gave a little curtsey, then led me back into the hall and along to a closed door near the porch. Before entering, she turned to face the hall and, putting a crooked finger behind her left ear, looked at me again, as if requiring some further recognition.

I listened carefully and, in the dim distance, detected the sound of a dog barking. Even though far away, the tone was distinctly aggressive and I surmised that it was a none-too pleased Mika, voicing her indignation at being separated from her young.

Again, confirming the arrangements with a nod and a little bob, she opened the door before us, to reveal a small washroom with a hand-basin and toilet. And on the floor between the two stood a large wicker basket containing six fat, snoozing Boxer pups.

It seemed rather incongruous, in a house of that style, to have no purpose-built kennel. Perhaps there might have been one somewhere, but when bitches make ready for whelping, they often choose the most unlikely places if allowed – and from the tone of Mika's bark, I concluded that if she chose the washroom, then washroom it was!

I decided to take the pups one at a time from their 'nursery-loo', into the dining-room in order to avoid any unnecessary disturbance to the litter and, scooping up the first of the warm, furry bundles, I returned to my mighty operating table. The task was simple: firstly I cut out the vestiges of the dew-claws on the inside of the paws with my curved scissors, after swabbing them with spirit. Whatever the arguments for or against tail-docking, the removal of these rudimentary 'thumbs' is quite acceptable, in my view. For they serve no useful purpose and even nature has attempted to phase them out, by preventing their contact with the ground. But if left hanging, they can become trapped or torn, causing unnecessary pain and distress.

The tails I amputated with a special pair of sterile nail clippers, which I found most useful for the purpose, as they cut on one side and sealed on the other. A squeeze, a twist, a little 'yelp' and it was all over. Some sulphonamide dressing and the first pup had had its 'topping and tailing' completed and was carried back across the hallway, to be replaced with its mates.

Old Mrs Jolokowski followed me back and forth like a little blackbird, but making no sound and showing no untoward reactions as the snow-white cloth on the oak table, became progressively blood spattered.

I did not take more than five or six minutes to do the lot, but as I proceeded, the squeaks and protests at the disturbance, coming from the 'nursery-loo', increased in volume and had become quite a racket when I crossed the hall with the last pup. It was then that I heard a door slamming somewhere in the house – the sharpness of the sound even stopped the pup squeaking and I momentarily halted in mid-stride. As I did, I glanced at old Mrs 'J', whose gentle grey eyes were now full of apprehension – her reasoning justified. For as if accompanied by a rushing wind, around the corner and onto the opposite end of the expensive Turkish runner came Mika – a hunk of seething muscle and blood, showing all the maternal anger of a distinctly upset mum!

She did not even stop to size up the situation: she just came, eyes flashing, jaws apart, snarling aggressively – a canine missile ready for 'take-off'!

And take off she did, a few yards from me. Before I had any chance to move.

It was the runner that saved me, for her hind legs slipped as she left the ground, reducing her force of propulsion: instead of hitting me full frontal, she came to one side and sank her teeth into my forearm. With the pup in my right hand I was absolutely defenceless, but I had the presence of mind to hold it aloft and to my right side.

The diversion caused her to let go. But only for an instant, for she rapidly recovered, ran back a few paces, turned and came at me again.

This time, I was ready.

Instinctively, I transferred the pup into my left hand, already part paralysed by the bite, and, as she rose in the air, I hit her with my clenched fist – right between the eyes!

I worried for a long time about that act. Hugh Lasgarn, dedicated vet, punching an animal with all the force he could muster. Defensive ... aggressive ... protective ... or was I just frightened!

Fright is a transient physiological reaction without which a vet, like a bat without its radar, could not exist. The bull that might charge; the horse that might kick; the cat that might scratch ... or, indeed, the bitch intent on tearing apart anyone who is mutilating her newborn – for whatever modish motives. All of them generate a degree of fright, which sharpens the senses, increases the awareness and summons up the extra strength needed to cope with such an unpredictable situation.

Ethics notwithstanding, it was a good clout and she dropped like a stone. But although my blow had stalled her, it had in no way reduced her venom or commitment. Before she could get to her feet again, I charged into the 'nursery-loo' with the pup and slammed the door.

Leaning against it, I added my support to the welcome barrier, as Mika battered relentlessly, like a starving wolf, at my sole defence. Only when I was satisfied it would hold, did I ease my weight.

It was then that I felt the pimples and the cold shudders

– the undetectable elements of fright. Suddenly, I sensed a great weakness coming over me and sat heavily and thankfully upon Mr Jolokowski's solid, well polished lavatory seat.

After a few minutes, I recovered my composure and lowered the pup, which was still clutched in my hand, down to its squeaking mates.

Mika was still making her presence felt, but I assumed that old Mrs Jolokowski would be able to distract her and return her to her original confinement. Then, I should be free.

After about five minutes the situation was unchanged. There had been two occasions when I timorously turned the door knob; each time Mika had responded in top form.

I shouted – but as I did so, I sensed the futility of my effort and was suddenly acutely aware that I, a qualified veterinary surgeon, with quite a bit of experience in mixed agricultural practice was, for my professional future and immediate personal safety, entirely dependent upon an aged expatriate Polish Granny.

The fact that she was deaf and spoke no English merely added to the complexity of the situation. I might as well have been in Poland – and with the aggressor being of German extraction, I could have sat and philosophised for some time.

However, it was no time for reflections: I abandoned thought and shouted for help.

It was rather naïve on my part to think that old Mrs Jolokowski would snap into action – although I did hope. But my exhortations fell upon stony ground. However, I persisted with various vocal suggestions about enticing Mika away with food, or opening the front door so that she might run into the garden. In that event, I could break out from the 'nursery-loo', but still have to make it to the car.

It was all to no avail. I examined the loo window, but one would have needed the expertise of Houdini to even contemplate squeezing through the gap, which was louvred and barely one foot across. I did have enough paper to make smoke signals – but no matches. So that was out!

I had no further ideas and in desperation I sat down again on the oak seat, remembering the days when I used to boisterously join in the rude song of 'Three old ladies, locked in the lavatory. They've been there from Monday to Saturday . . . de, dah, de, dah'.

Well, it was now Wednesday, and my old lady was free on the other side of the door. All in all, I did not find it very funny.

My left arm, the one that had taken the full force of Mika's onslaught, was beginning to throb, so I took off my shirt to inspect the damage. Both left canine teeth had struck home, leaving two deep puncture wounds, fore and aft. Though filled with blood, they were not haemorrhaging excessively, but painful and the muscle was beginning to stiffen.

Damn dog's tails, I thought, beginning to feel a bit evil myself and remembering the Wang episode. No doubt Confucius had a maxim for this one, too.

The next hour consisted of Mika barking, snarling and scratching at the door, and me shouting, listening, swearing and using the loo. On two occasions I heard old Mrs Jolokowski's voice – she was saying something like, 'Dobra. Dobra Mika' – which I hoped was an effort to calm down the still frantic bitch. But even that hope faded when I heard her shuffle away.

I had suggested she rang my surgery, forgetting that she spoke no English, and at one point had pushed the instructions under the door on a piece of paper, with a drawing of a telephone and the number – but from the sound of the 'noises off', Mika inconsiderately made a meal of it!

By now, daylight was fading and I pulled on the light switch. The bulb shone brightly, then spluttered, spat . . . and died! I was going to be in the dark as well.

I sat upon my throne once more and shook my head disconsolately.

Five minutes later, I had another bright idea. If I opened the door a trifle – not wide enough for Mika to get in – I might be able to push the pups out one at a time, so pacifying her.

My efforts nearly ended in disaster and injury to my other arm, for the pups were fat and awkward, and Mika only too ready to take revenge on any of my extremities.

At six o'clock, having been incarcerated for nearly three hours, I decided the whole situation was farcical: I was going to have to make a break for it. I settled upon another ruse. Taking off my shirt, I tied the open end of one sleeve in a knot and stuffed two hand-towels, of which there were several, down inside. The strategy was to make a false arm, which I could offer to Mika as I made my break. She would go for it and, as she did so, if I threw it back into the washroom behind me, she would follow it, I would slam the door – and Bob's your uncle!

'Lasgarn, you're brilliant,' I said to myself, as shades of 'Escape from Colditz' and 'The Wooden Horse', flitted through my mind.

But the arm was too short when stuffed. And filling the whole shirt made it too bulky. For safety, the distraction had to be long, in order to keep Mika at bay. If a sleeve was too short, there was only one other way.

It was a long shot – but it worked!

Ten minutes later, I was on my way home and, as I drove along, the draught sneaking uncomfortably up the legs of my underpants, I wondered how Diana would react when I explained that I had had to stuff my trousers with towels to distract an angry bitch – or would she just put her arm round me and say once again, 'Hugh, you're working too hard!'

Mr Jolokowski was very apologetic when he heard the news, graciously asking me to replace my shirt and trousers at his expense. My arm remained painful for several days but Diana, though concerned about my injury, continued for some time to enquire about the appearance of the Polish Granny!

\*    \*    \*

In retrospect, the reactions of Mika, and even of Diana, were, I suppose, understandable, yet they also demonstrated the vagaries and indeed the unpredictability of the female mind.

'All to do with hormones,' McBean, my Irish colleague, would say dismissively, whenever an irate lady client or his longstanding and vivacious girlfriend, Mimi Lafont, created a scene. In fact his pontifications on the fair sex and the reasons for their actions and reactions, were boundless. And perhaps his constant theorising accounted for his persistent bachelor state, despite Mimi's attractions. 'Get married when I'm good and ready,' he would say, with a wink. 'Good enough now. But just not ready!'

Sam Juggins was another confirmed bachelor. A likeable rogue was Sam, who had once come to my aid during a market dispute in which I had to arbitrate, when I first came to Ledingford.

He farmed a small-holding just on the outskirts of the town, doing a bit of cattle dealing on the side. Situated as he was, only half a mile from the market, he could easily pop home if the trade was good and bring in a few head of stock, or conversely, at the close of the day when the trade was down, he would buy up the tail-enders, taking them home until it picked up again, when back they would come.

He had purchased a bunch of pregnant Friesian heifers, intending to calve them down and sell them 'fresh' in the Dairy Sale. Sam had positive thoughts on most things and I can picture him now, standing in the pouring rain, tugging at his red neck-a-chief – as much a part of him as Mr Wang's hat – wiping the mud from his eyes with his crumpled cap and commenting wryly:

'There ain't no understandin' wimin an' weather!'

Whilst the weather at that precise moment needed no qualification, Sam had included with 'wimin' one of his young heifers, to whom we had just given assistance in the production of her bull calf.

He was a large calf, even for a Friesian, and had unfortunately stuck at the hips after coming most of the way quite easily, by himself. When I arrived following Sam's urgent call, he was hanging halfway out of the mother's womb and bawling for attention.

'Tried a bit o' weight on 'is legs,' said Sam, 'but 'im's tight – an' she's small, anyway. Bloke who put 'im there ought to come an' get 'im away, I say!' he added, shaking his head.

Stripping off and donning my red rubber apron, I attached some cotton calving ropes to the protruding forelegs, whilst the little heifer stood impassively, back arched from the weight of her offspring's dangling body.

'Shoved some "marg" round 'im, an' all,' said Sam, pointing to the messy remains on the windowsill. 'That's best, ain't it?'

Sam was right, for margarine, being of primarily vegetable origin, absorbed less rapidly than animal fats, its effect lasting longer and making it preferable to many other lubricants. Although I remember once asking for some, whilst calving a cow at Mrs Williams' of Pontavon, over by the Black Mountain. Tommy, her son, who was helping me, ran to the house to get it and returned instead with a beautifully presented pat of home-made butter.

'Margarine, I wanted, Tom,' I said.

'That's what I asked for,' he replied. 'But Mam told me off; said what will you think of us, giving you margarine, and that only butter was good enough for you.'

Another gracious, but typically feminine conclusion.

However, Sam's heifer, despite the 'marg' and considerable traction, would not produce and we both pulled ourselves close to exhaustion. The heifer, who was tied by the horns, had given up trying long before and, apart from remaining in the standing position, which was some advantage, did little else to assist.

Finally, I decided to see if I could rotate the half-born bull by tying both forelegs together, then passing a calving stick through the knot and twisting the body like a corkscrew. This had the effect of turning it through 360 degrees in the hope that, at some point, the pattern of its hips would fit the gap in its mother's pelvis more closely – rather like one of those frustrating Christmas puzzles!

To my delight and relief, it worked. The calf suddenly eased forward and, with a thankful heave from the heifer, he slid into my arms and I gently lowered his 'marg' anointed body to the floor. The heifer straightened her back and shook herself, glad it was all over.

'Phew!' exclaimed Sam. 'What a pantomime!'

Kneeling down, I removed part of the membrane sticking to the young calf's coat and cleared his mouth and nostrils, so that he could inhale his first breaths of country air, whilst the heifer looked round at him adoringly.

'There,' I said to her. 'You've got a fine young son to be proud of – worth the effort for all of us. Eh Sam?'

Sam, still puffing after his exertions, nodded, and I went forward to untie the rope securing her horns. She flicked her ear as I freed her, then, turning a trifle stiffly toward her newborn, lowered her head and licked his coat tentatively with her long pink tongue.

'There's something so fundamental about motherhood,' I remarked to Sam, as we both stood back and took in the happy scene. But my choice of words was rather unfortunate, for no sooner had I uttered my philosophical observation than the heifer looked up, her eyes wild and staring, snorted furiously and came at us both with horns lowered!

It was my fundament that got it first, then Sam's as we turned for the door. We managed to get through, slamming it behind us, but in our haste to escape I slipped on some of the margarine and my feet went flying, tripping Sam in turn, so that we both fell in a heap in the mire. And just at that moment, completely without any warning – down came the rain!

⋆   ⋆   ⋆

There was a lot to be said for Sam's observations about 'wimin' and weather', and many are the times that I have been caught out by both.

Not least at Little Cwm Twt.

The place was an isolated farmhouse, stone built and standing rather dejectedly in a fold of the valley, from which it took its name. It had been taken over by a group of Hippies, known locally and somewhat scathingly as the 'Funny Folk'.

They seemed to survive by the grace of God and some earthly supplementation from the State, the latter being the only reason they were ever seen amongst work-a-day mortals, when they came to collect their benefits. The men were gaunt and hairy, the women pale, dreamy and uncannily attractive, their livelihood being maintained by basic line agriculture.

Peculiar breeds of pigs, sheep and poultry roamed the farmstead, the like of which local stockmen had never seen. The plants in their garden, too, were of varieties that defied normal botanical identification.

I had received a message, left at the surgery on the back of one of Her Majesty's brown, window-type envelopes. It was written in beautiful copperplate hand and stated, in the briefest possible terms, that my services were required to minister to the needs of a sick goat.

It was late afternoon when I managed to get to Little Cwm Twt and was a mite annoyed at having to leave my car at the bottom of the rutted lane. Lugging my medical case over the muddy tracks generated an uncomfortable warmth, for though the day had started with a sharp, frost-chilled morning, the sun now beamed down strongly and I still had vest, shirt, Guernsey and anorak about my body.

So much for understanding the weather!

The farmhouse stood sombre and aloof at the edge of a stonewalled yard, empty but for some broken wooden barrels, half a dozen bantams and a clapped-out ex-WD Austin Seven coupé, the original khaki having been over-painted in an explosion of psychedelic colour which, had it been present in wartime, would have dazzled the enemy for miles around!

The weatherbeaten, solid oak door of the dwelling was flanked by windows sheeted with corrugated tin and, whilst all was silent save for the squabbling of the bantams, a sweetness pervaded the still air, which was pleasing to my nostrils.

As I stood before the crumbling edifice, hot and flustered, I noticed the door had no bell or knocker, so I hammered upon the woodwork with an old plough point that I found rusting on an adjacent windowsill.

An eerie quiet followed my efforts, but as I stood back, raising my head to survey the upper storeys, the door, without noise, swung slowly open.

A girl, tall, with long blonde hair, confronted me; save for a minuscule apology for a skirt around her slim waist, she stood before me naked to the tips of her toes!

A dying goldfish could not have looked more stupefied as my heart thumped, pulse raced and suddenly my case seemed to become very heavy.

'Oh! The vet!' she exclaimed, smiling sweetly, without the slightest trace of embarrassment. 'I'll go and get something on.'

The door closed as silently as it had opened, and I looked about for somewhere to sit down – but there was nowhere. When eventually she did return, I wished I had found somewhere for I really did need some support.

She certainly did have 'something on': a pair of black rubber wellington boots!

'Follow me,' she said, alluringly – and took me to see her goat.

The goat had been eating rhubarb leaves which, due to their high oxalic acid content, cause problems, as I explained to the nymph.

'You see, the acid combines with the body, body,' I said, trying to look at her without actually looking. She smiled. 'Body, body?' she questioned. 'Sorry, I mean "body cal-

34

cium",' I stuttered. 'The goat's body calcium, which affects its eyes . . . I mean, its eyes and muscles and . . . its body.'

'How about its milk?' she asked, breathing in unnecessarily deeply.

'Milk,' I said. 'Yes, milk. Yes, it will affect the milk.'

'How?' she persisted.

'How,' I replied. 'How.' She smiled and nodded, glad that she had made herself understood. 'Yes, well, there won't be any – for a while anyway. And then there'll be some again.'

She nodded and, before she could ask any further questions, I tore myself away and gave the goat its injections. The effect was quite rapid: its shivering and incoordination ceased and its eyes became less glazed.

Which is more than I could say for myself!

If the goat made the mistake of eating rhubarb leaves, I made the mistake of telling McBean about the incident when we met for an end-of-day pint in the Hopman.

He in turn, in a jocular mood some time later, told Diana – something that I had 'forgotten' to do.

Sam's 'wimin an' weather' proverb became reality once more and, although I was to be very much at the mercy of the elements in the near future; Diana's reaction was quite a hefty storm in itself!

# 4

Chance, fate or the 'Devil's Luck', call it what you will, but my life so far seemed to have been governed by a series of happenings not motivated consciously by myself.

There was the air raid, back in the 'forties, that gave me leave from Abergranog Primary School to take a short-cut home through Little Pant Farm, where I came across my first calving case. The fantastic experience so imprinted itself upon my youthful mind that it undoubtedly became one of the factors influencing my path into the veterinary profession. Then there was Boggy, my beloved first cat, which I fished out of the stinking Avon Llwyd. Through Boggy I learned to respect animals, discover what real companions they could be and know the heart-rending sadness when they die or are killed.

My coming to Ledingford in the first instance was another turn of fate, a chance discovery on the college notice board; and the death of Mr G. R. Hacker, the senior partner, turned my temporary assistantship into an extended stay. Then came the supreme chance of them all when, after a party, I was asked if I would give a lift to the girl whom I had thought by far the most attractive there. And that was how I met Diana.

Once again, it was a quirk of circumstance that was to lead me into a further and unexpected phase in my veterinary career, far from the green pastures; an opportunity not only to see the world but, through the cattle that I had worked with and come to respect so much, to meet new and interesting people.

I became a transit vet for the Hereford Cattle Society.

My 'chance' came when Bob Hacker broke his arm, after

a horse he was examining for a client lashed out and fractured his radius in two places.

I remember that day so clearly. He was sitting in his office, resting the new plaster cast on the desk.

'Got a moment, Hugh?' he called.

I went through and sat on the window-sill overlooking the garden, a spot I seemed to have claimed as my own, whenever we had a practice meeting or discussion. McBean usually took the only other chair, as he was doing on that occasion.

'I'm crocked!' exclaimed Bob, thumping the cast on the wooden rim of the desk, 'and only half a bloke for the next six weeks.'

'We can manage,' I said, looking at McBean.

Bob looked at me and smiled. 'No, Hugh. *We* can manage,' he replied, nodding towards his partner. 'I want you to go to Finland.'

I did not answer for a few seconds, then just said, 'Finland', as if I did not know where or what it was.

'Yes, Finland,' said Bob. 'Land of a Thousand Lakes! Saunas! Reindeers! Father Christmas! I want you to go with the Herefords.'

I nodded, as if I had previously understood. 'What about you, Mac?' I said. 'Don't you want to go?'

McBean gave his beard a rub against the grain, then shook his head sagely. 'Well, now,' he said, 'I only like water when it's with whisky – and then, not too much of it.'

I had known for some time that the shipment was in the offing, but Bob Hacker was seeing to all the veterinary arrangements for the Society and so I had had little to do with it, except to read some of the progress reports I saw from time to time on his desk. To me there was something quite exciting in just reading them – never contemplating, in my wildest dreams, that I would become more closely involved.

I had met the Finnish buyers, though again quite by chance, on a routine visit to Paxton at Donhill. He bred some of the finest Herefords in the county, with bloodlines going back as far as the 1800s and the Grove family, which were among the first Herefords ever to be exported to America.

Paxton had introduced me to the group, fighting shy of pronouncing their names, just calling them 'these good gentlemen from Finland'. Paxton could always shelve his natural arrogance and aggression, to which I was well accustomed, if there was a deal in the offing. But once the fish was hooked, he would soon revert to type.

There were three 'good gentlemen from Finland', although only one seemed to do any talking. He was the stockiest of the trio, bareheaded, sporting a heavy black overcoat and a thick woollen scarf; of his companions, one was similarly dressed, but the other wore a coat of leather, long and black, with great, flat lapels and a wide belt. He was bespectacled and wore upon his head a homburg and, whilst all three appeared of serious disposition, he seemed possessed of a distinctly mysterious air.

After the introductions and unsolicited camaraderie, Paxton added to the patriarchal atmosphere by putting a hand on my shoulder – something completely unprecedented – and saying grandly:

'Lasgarn, here, will vouch for the health and fitness of my cattle.'

'Vouching won't be necessary,' said the stocky one in a positive, clipped tone. 'If they pass the required tests, that will be quite satisfactory.'

His manner was polite but firm and I remember thinking, as his steel-grey eyes fixed me squarely, that whoever he was, he was going to be a good match for the old man. For Paxton enjoyed confrontation and often went out of his way to provoke it; many were the battles I had had with the old buzzard since I had come to Ledingford – though to be fair, now that I was more established, I enjoyed the encounters and could give as good as I got.

'They'll pass! They'll pass!' he shouted, banging his silver-topped cane sharply on the ground, at which the Finns remained impassive.

'What are the requirements?' I asked, feeling I should close ranks with him a little.

The Finn who had so far done all the talking proceeded to rattle off the conditions:

'Good conformation and freedom from any weakness, deformity or hereditary ailment, with particular attention being payed to hips, jaw-lines, eyes, teat structure in females and testicles in males. Ages to be certified, together with an assurance as to normal general health and well-being – this to be confirmed within twenty-four hours of transit. Absolute freedom from infectious and contagious disease, from parasites, both internal and external.' Without even appearing to take a breath, he continued his chronicle of requirements, his eyes hardly blinking as he spoke, and just the slightest suggestion of a smile appearing at the corners of his mouth, as if to say, 'You ask – I tell you!'

Paxton, meanwhile, persistently tapped his cane, rather irritably, obviously feeling a little out of his depth – something he never relished. The Finn continued: 'A tuberculosis test will be carried out, first on the premises of origin, then in quarantine, the readings to conform with the existing UK standards. Blood tests will also be required for brucellosis, leptospirosis and enzootic bovine leucosis . . .' At this point, Paxton could contain himself no longer.

'S'pose you want them bloody gift-wrapped as well!' he snapped. The Finn, however, ignored his comment.

'We would just like the bulls tested for fertility and the females to be guaranteed pregnant.' He then put his hands together in the manner of a priest and permitted himself to develop his secret smile. 'One final request,' he added. 'We wish them to be of good temperament – no wild animals, please.'

'Good temperament is something for which Herefords are renowned,' I countered, feeling that I, too, had been given a lecture.

'Then there is no problem,' the Finn conceded smoothly. 'No problem at all.'

There was no doubt Paxton was disturbed by the ice-cool attitude on display, together with the underlying assertion that, no matter what we thought of our cattle, they were not taking our word for it and were leaving nothing to chance.

'Bloody distrusting bunch of foreigners!' he roared, after they had disappeared down the long driveway. 'Good mind not to sell them any at all!'

But I knew this last statement to be far from the truth.

Paxton was a self-made man who had risen from humble origins; I knew quite a lot about him, having seen him in all moods, from violent rages to the heartbreaking occasion when his aviary had been plundered and his beautiful birds horrendously butchered.

Despite his success, he was not a happy man. Though his farming estate was one of the show-pieces for many a mile, he still carried a large chip on his stooping shoulders as not being truly accepted into the County class structure. So a chance to sell his cattle abroad was, for him, more than just a commercial transaction, but another shot at his goal of compatability with the many gentry who were members of the Society at the time.

However, subject to passing all tests, the Finns wished to purchase from him ten heifers, due to calve in three months, and one bull, a two-year-old. They had all passed with flying colours and were now quarantined on Ministry of Agriculture premises with the rest of the consignment of seventy-nine heifers and four bulls, two of which were reserves.

My contact with the Finns had been fairly fleeting, so the somewhat sinister impression I had gathered of them had not concerned me at all. But now that I realised I was going to be very much involved, those cold, steel-grey eyes of the stocky Nordic spokesman kept flashing through my mind.

Bob Hacker may well have anticipated my thoughts.

'It's a tough one, Hugh,' he commented. 'No picnic – and those Finns are no pushover. Their eyes may be sunk a bit deep in their heads, but they don't miss many tricks. Anyway, go and see Ernie Shelton; he's the Export Manager at the Society. He'll tell you all you want to know. Half of the cattle are from our practice, anyway. Paxton's got a bunch going – one of his bulls, too: Donhill Porchester.' Bob got up from his desk rather stiffly. 'Donhill Porchester,' he repeated. 'Watch him – he's just like his owner. A real bastard!'

But Donhill Porchester's particular idiosyncrasies did not worry me, for I was already fired by the excitement of the 'chance' and, after fixing up to see Ernie Shelton the following morning, I sped home to tell Diana the good news.

She was coming back from the shops when I pulled up outside our semi on the Belbury Road; it was a practice house but only a few years old and quite pleasant. Sara, our first daughter, was just eleven months old and fast asleep in her pram. I left the car and went to meet them.

Motherhood had given Diana a glow that only enhanced her youthful beauty – still to me as radiant as when I had first met my 'girl on the piano stool' so fortuitously, at that party. I had marked her down then as the best-looking girl I had ever seen – and I still thought so.

'You're early!' she said. 'I was going to be back before you.'

I kissed her and put my hand on the pram handle. 'You look rather pleased with yourself,' she went on, then she took a step backwards and studied me enquiringly with her deep blue eyes. 'What's going on?'

'I'm going to sea,' I said, putting my arm round her. 'Me and about eighty Herefords. Di – I'm going to Finland!'

She did not say anything at all for several seconds; then she took a little breath and bit her lip gently as the corner.

'Aren't you pleased?' I asked.

She nodded, trying to force a smile, but the tears, which were only a blink away, got there first.

'Don't you want me to go?'

She nodded again, this time the smile coming through the glistening tear drops, then she put up her hand, squeezed the back of my neck and said, softly, 'Darling. You'd better get your hair cut.'

I had been so full of eager anticipation about the trip that I had not honestly considered Diana's reaction, more or less assuming that she would go along with the idea – which indeed, she had. Although we had been married for nearly two years and had a lovely daughter, I never felt at any time 'tied' – that is with family responsibilities. But nevertheless, they were there all the same and this opportunity had suddenly brought them more into focus. There was danger in the trip, of that there was no doubt – that was part of the attraction – and crossing the Baltic in March would be some boat-ride. I could, of course, turn it down; no doubt the Society would find someone, somewhere – but I really was keen to go.

However, if Di had done anything to dampen my initial euphoria, it was only due to her care and concern for my safety; something for which I counted myself, as Paxton had once observed, 'a very lucky man'.

\* \* \*

Ernie Shelton was small and dapper, a Londoner who had come to the Society after many years in the shipping business. His office was large and airy, situated on the top floor of Hereford House and overlooking the Ledingford skyline. The morning I met him, it had been raining and the ancient rooftops glistened in the watery sunshine. A secretary had escorted me in, to find him poring over a great pile of papers on his desk.

'Won't keep you a jiff,' he cracked. 'Take a seat!'

I did so and, while I waited, took in the array of pictures of ships that lined the walls. There were some magnificent vessels amongst them: mostly white, with clean, fine lines, ploughing majestically through calm seas and blue skies, dappled with fluffy white clouds running away to the far horizons behind them. 'A sailor's life for me,' I thought, and turned my attention back to Ernie Shelton at his desk.

Eventually, the little man took off his glasses and placed them carefully on the polished surface; then, standing up, he stretched rather uncomfortably across the desk and offered me his hand.

'Hugh Lasgarn, our new vet, eh! Ernie Shelton!'

Formalities completed, he sat back in his chair and reached for a huge pipe, lying at the ready in an ashtray. It was already primed and, before making any further comment, he lit it and disappeared, almost instantaneously and completely from my sight, in a cloud of thick, blue smoke.

I was forced to clear my throat several times, but when Ernie Shelton reappeared from the noxious pall, he seemed bright-eyed and completely unaffected.

It was only then that he took the instrument from his mouth and held it aloft, still belching smoke: 'Don't mind, do you?' he asked. 'Been at it since I was seven – me ole Mum taught me!' Then, he gave a gnomish chuckle and sat up straight. 'Right, Hugh! What do you know about shipping livestock?'

'Not a lot,' I admitted. 'Well, to be perfectly honest – nothing!'

'Nothing,' he repeated rather speculatively, and sank back into his chair and fell silent.

'Well, I am the reserve,' I countered, after a while.

Ernie Shelton suddenly broke from his brief reverie, took the pipe from his mouth and pointed the stem towards me:

'Reserve you may be, Hugh Lasgarn. But listen to me and survive this trip – and you'll be captaining the first team next time.'

'*Survive!*' I spluttered, quite involuntarily.

'Well, it won't be a picnic, that's for sure,' he chuckled. 'But we haven't lost a vet at sea yet – d'ye drink tea?' I nodded. 'I'll ring for some,' he said with a grin, obviously aware of my reaction. 'Looks as if you could do with it!'

Tea arrived, rather incongruously, in two large, white mugs.

'Relic of my shipping days,' he said. 'Can't get used to cups – and the tea is made to my instructions. If the spoon won't stand up in it, it isn't tea, is it?'

It certainly was a potent brew and, combined with the voluminous pipe smoke and the seafaring pictures, the office began to take on the atmosphere of a dockside pub, not unlike the Black Lion in Newpool, which I remembered from my student days with C.J., my mentor when 'seeing practice'. In no way was it the style that the prestigious Society premises, known by some as 'The Embassy', attempted to engender.

But it showed Ernie Shelton as a realist, a man who, over the coming years, I was to discover as a dynamic personality, and who possessed Napoleonic characteristics, befitting his small stature.

'Shipping cattle,' he expounded, 'is like bell-ringing. There are a dozen bloody ropes and only a couple of ringers – and before you get a decent tune, you can make a hell of a lot of clangers!' With that truism, he dispensed with his pipe, replacing it in the ashtray. 'Right,' he continued. 'Ropes pulled so far! All the cattle – that's seventy-nine pregnant heifers and four bulls – are in quarantine at Worlton, near Ross, in premises approved by the Ministry of Agriculture and under their complete supervision. They have all passed the tests and, subject to final approval as to health status and fitness to travel, which will be your responsibility, are ready to sail on Wednesday next. Certification is complete, transport arranged, bills of lading organised and, weather permitting, the *Dagmar Hansen*, your ship, now in Belfast, will be in Newpool Docks at 0.600 hours on that date.'

He sat up straight and shook his head, like a little cock pheasant asserting his patch, and eyed me questioningly. I nodded as if I was in full agreement, though in truth, a slight degree of misgiving was setting in – there was more to this cattle job than I had appreciated.

Ernie set off again, 'Right,' he said, 'that's the ones I've pulled – now for yours. Firstly, the cattle.' He pushed across to me the great pile of papers he had been studying when I arrived. 'Owners. Earmarks. Ages and Breeding. Certification next.' He pushed another wadge of paper forward. 'Blood tests, tuberculin charts, pregnancy and fertility guarantees. These . . .' he thumped his hand on the last pile to emphasise his point. 'These you must check – if they're wrong, you, my lad, are in the firing line!' I nodded again, but this time not very convincingly. 'Drink your tea,' he said, noticing my apprehension. 'It'll get cold.' So I took another swig of 'sailor's' tea, to steady my nerves.

'Second rope: fodder. Tell me what you want and I'll order it.'

Tell him what I wanted – I hadn't a clue! What would seventy-nine heifers and two bulls consume on a cruise to Finland? Did they lose their appetite, as many humans would, or eat their heads off in the sea air?

'What's the normal ration?' I asked, hopefully disguising my ignorance.

Ernie obviously knew, so why the estimation was left to me, I could not guess. 'Hay and broad bran,' he said. 'Take some cubes if you like, but they won't eat it. Work on about seven pounds of hay daily for the heifers and two of bran; double for small bulls and treble for large. And don't forget to add on at least three extra days, for rough weather. Anyway, go down to Worlton an' look 'em over tomorrow; you can work out the grub then.'

'It'll be on the dockside before loading, when you must approve it – just in case it poisons 'em all at sea . . . then you might as well jump over the side, yourself!'

So that was why I was responsible for the fodder – and I began to think that the last rope in Ernie's analogy would be the one around my neck. 'What drugs shall I need?' I asked.

Ernie Shelton picked up his pipe again and coughed. 'You're the vet, Hugh!' he said, quite sharply. Then he eased his manner. 'The vet, steward, nursemaid, diplomat and trouble-shooter.'

'Is that all?' I said, by now feeling distinctly uneasy

about the job specification and the unforeseen responsibilities.

'Don't look so glum,' Ernie comforted, standing up and offering his hand again. 'You'll enjoy it!'

But as I left the Society building that morning, I already had my doubts.

That night, I went through the list. The consignment had been drawn from a wide area of the Borders: from Breconshire, the Black Mountains, across to Belbury country and down as far as the lower Wye Valley.

There were quite a few cattle from our own clients. Paxton, of course, with Donhill Porchester, and two others that also gave me particular pleasure to see – the Payne brothers of Wormcastle and Howell Powell.

Howell Powell farmed on the slopes of the Black Mountain, his windswept acres carrying a flock of Welsh sheep and a small herd of Herefords. A bachelor, he lived alone and, to a great extent, treated any ailing livestock himself, with commonsense stockmanship and a bit of folk medicine thrown in – a feature I had already experienced with his 'sod treatment' for 'foul of the foot'.

Due to his degree of self-sufficiency in veterinary matters, visits were rare. On one occasion, however, when he was due to pay his bill, which he did with great fuss and commotion, he asked me into his house. It was quite a surprise, not only to be invited over his threshold, but to find that, although Howell farmed in such wild country, 'dog and stick' fashion, with a minimum of farm maintenance – string and six-inch nails being the extent of repairs – the interior of his dwelling was in considerable contrast. For whilst he lived frugally, his furniture and fittings were elegant and well kept, no doubt having been handed down over the years.

The kitchen was low-beamed and bright, with a magnificent oak Welsh dresser against one wall, on which stood a fine china dinner service. And on the top, a line of lustre jugs that made the eyes pop. A great oak table, with chairs to match, silverware and several paintings of Hereford cattle enriched the remainder of the room.

But of all the beautiful things, the one that intrigued me most was a copper kettle. It was not large and neither did it appear heavy, but I found its shape fascinating. The body was somewhat square, rather like a saucepan, the opening rimmed delicately with brass. The handle was curved, partly brass, partly copper, and the spout had a certain elegance that reminded me of an Indian dancer.

While he fumbled away in a drawer for his cheque book, I remarked, quite innocently, what a beautiful kettle it was.

Howell Powell ceased ferreting amongst the papers and, turning his head, retorted brusquely: 'It is! An you 'ent the first one to fancy that, neither!' as if I had been trying to beg it. So I never mentioned it again, just admired it in silence.

It was at the Ministry Tuberculin Test, some time later, that Howell's problem came to light. Although he did not have much faith in vets, he lost no opportunity in picking the brains of any of us whenever he could – especially when, as on Ministry business, the visit did not cost him anything. As we caught, haltered and tested the Herefords, he admitted that he was unhappy about their general condition.

'Never could get no "bloom" on 'em, even in gran'father's day,' he told me. 'They goes off this time o' year, when they should be lookin' well. I treats 'em for the worms, feeds 'em good an' gives 'em all sorts – but they just don't do.'

As we worked through the bunch, measuring, injecting and recording the ear numbers, I took a careful look at each one. They certainly did not appear to be as thriving as most other Herefords in the county, for their coats were rough and their bodies slack.

'I was thinkin' to change the bull,' said Howell. 'P'r'aps the breeding's gone wrong.'

'Before you do that,' I suggested, 'let me take a few blood samples.'

'What'll that cost me?' he retorted immediately.

'It will be worth it,' I replied. 'I think your cattle have got a mineral deficiency.'

What made me suspicious was the colour of their coats, the red texture in many areas developing a yellow tinge. Around the eyes, the lighter hairs stood out in rings, giving the appearance of spectacles.

Saying that as long as it did not bankrupt him, he was prepared to let me take the bloods, he agreed. In due course the laboratory results confirmed my suspicions: Howell Powell's cattle were suffering from copper deficiency.

I treated the whole herd and told him that if it was done regularly, his stock would improve no end – which indeed it did.

Then, one Wednesday – market day – there came a parcel to the surgery.

'Mr Powell from Glan-Nant left this for you,' said Miss Billings, our receptionist, and handed me an odd-shaped parcel, covered in brown paper and tied with string. By the very feel of it, I knew exactly what it was and did not open it until I got home.

Then, with great pride and a bit of a lump in my throat, I unwrapped the copper kettle and put it on my sideboard.

The other name that caught my eye, suitably apt in the circumstances, was Wormcastle Lucky Chance, a yearling bull from Reg and Harry Payne – a son of Wormcastle Hugh, with whom I had very special connections.

It was shortly after I had become engaged to Diana that I was called to a late-night calving at Wormcastle; the heifer was small and tight, the calf too large. Diana had come with me, just for company, but finished up helping to perform a caesarian operation and produce a fine young bull. It was the first I had done without any supervision and a unique, even magical experience for us both.

But three days later the heifer died, leaving the little calf an orphan and Diana and myself devastated.

A post mortem examination revealed it was inevitable, for she had a longstanding deformity of the aorta, which ruptured under the stress – something that would have happened shortly anyway. Even so, it was little consolation and I took it badly for some time.

Reg and Harry were very generous in their condolences to me, though they had suffered the actual loss. But they were two of 'nature's gentlemen' and I thought a lot of them both. And when they called the little orphan after me, despite the tragedy, I was deeply touched.

So, to see Hugh's progeny, now eligible for international honours, was greatly rewarding; there was one disappointment, however: 'Lucky Chance' was only a reserve and though he had passed all his tests, it did not look as if his prospects were going to live up to his name.

The Quarantine Station was situated in spacious, modern farm buildings a few miles south of Ross. They had been necessary, for although several ports had isolation facilities, Newpool did not, so the premises at Worlton had been selected. Due to a change in the owner's policy to arable farming, the unit had held no cattle for twelve months, hence its approval by the Ministry.

They, in turn, supervised the running of the place and left the visitor in no doubt that they did so. Every hundred yards or so, running from the main road and up the drive to the yard area, were posted notices a yard square saying in large, black lettering: 'MINISTRY OF AGRICULTURE QUARANTINE STATION – KEEP OUT!'

However, at the yard gate next to one of these formal proclamations, was a smaller, better-tempered announcement, written in longhand on a card, which said: 'Please ring for attention!' The bell sitting on the wall above it was a large brass model with a black handle, as used by town criers, auctioneers or oldfashioned school marms.

Grasping it firmly, I shook the clapper and produced a

sound that would have wakened the dead – and, under normal circumstances, stampeded any cattle for miles around.

As the jangling echoes pierced the barns, an apparition appeared from a small wooden hut sited on the inside, a few yards away. He looked like an advertisement for Skipper Sardines, with long black rubber waders, voluminous mackintosh and a great sou'wester, which came well down over his ears. He raised his hand in silent salute, then, still without a word and as if performing some ceremonial rite, lifted up a black bucket that was standing by the shed door and poured the contents all down his front!

For a few seconds he stood there, as if waiting for some magical transformation to take place – but I could tell by the smell that it was Jeyes Fluid and not likely to alter his state in any way, other than to make him smell highly sanitary and drip little pools of white liquid onto the floor, about his person.

Then continuing the pantomime, he took down a brush that had been hanging by a string above the bucket and gave himself three swipes across his chest, like a Freemason; then – only then – did he come forward.

'Hugh Lasgarn,' I announced. 'I'm going with the cattle.'

The walking antiseptic set his forehead in a deep frown, then turned on his rubber heels and disappeared again into the wooden hut, to emerge almost immediately with a clipboard, which he studied intently. Twice he looked up at me and then back to the board. Eventually, seemingly satisfied with my identification, he came back to the gate and held out a smelly, sticky, Jeyes Fluid-fresh hand over the gate:

'Clarry Norris,' he said. 'OVO!' – which was not the password, but his Ministry designation of Official Veterinary Officer.

'Right, I'll get my coat,' I suggested, now that I accepted that even I had been officially 'vetted'.

But his reaction startled me, for he ripped his hand

away, as if he had touched a red-hot Aga, and let out a great 'Aarrhh!' like one mortally wounded.

I ducked instinctively, in case any more missiles were in transit. 'What's the matter?' I yelled.

'No, laddie. No! Ye canna dae tha'!' he cried out, in pure Glaswegian. 'Ye must ha' yin o' mine!'

A smile crept over my face at his response; of course, I had forgotten that all boots and clothing at quarantine must remain on the station and nothing from outside be brought in, a necessary precaution against the transmission of new infection after the cattle had been declared free of disease. But my amusement stemmed not only from his dialect, which I had not heard so authentically spoken since my Glasgow University days, but from what he had said – 'Ye must ha' yin o' mine!' – and from the memory of the night of my motorbike ride through that great and colourful city.

There had been a dance at the Student's Union and I had met a girl who lived at Cathcart, on the south side of the river. I had taken her back to Glasgow Cross to get the last bus, intending to walk back the three miles to my digs. It was not the first time I had legged it through the empty streets in the wee hours and I was keeping an eye out for the maintenance tram wagons; they could provide illicit transport if boarded from behind. Then suddenly the traffic lights, where I had halted, changed to red.

I was about to cross when a chap wearing an ex-army greatcoat, elbow-length black gauntlets and a khaki balaclava, pulled up alongside on a spluttering old AJS motorbike.

'Does ye wan' a lift?' he shouted.

'Where are you going?' I asked.

'Where d'ye wan'?' he yelled back.

'Anniesland!'

'Jump orn!'

I was in two minds about accepting, when the lights changed.

'Jump orn! I'll tak ye's!' he shouted through his woolly

helmet. So jump on I did and away we roared up Sauchie-hall Street.

There was no foot-rest on the right side, so I had to hold one leg in the air. My phantom chauffeur was crouched ahead, like a competitor in a Manx TT race, and as we rattled over cobbles and tram-lines, the wind streaming through my hair, I wondered where I would end up.

We sped through the night like two bats out of hell and it was a blessing the place was deserted, because we were using all the road – but eventually we arrived at Annies-land Cross and he pulled up against the pavement edge. Thankful for the lift and even more grateful for my sur-vival, I dismounted. My newfound friend dismounted also and pulled his bike up onto its stand. Then he fished deeply into his greatcoat pocket and pulled out a half-bottle of whisky.

'Tak a dram wi' me,' he offered. His generosity was quite remarkable and although I attempted to decline, he insisted, so I did and thanked him profusely.

'Dinna' fash yersel',' he said, taking a swig himself. 'We're hospitable folk in Glasgae.'

'You certainly are,' I agreed sincerely.

'Dae ye's know,' he said, passing the bottle back, 'I'll tell ye's aboot Glasgae hospitality.

'Ye's can be standin' on the corner of a street on a cold wintry night, an' a fella can pull up in his car an' say: "Hey! You'se canna staun' there in the cauld and wet aw'night – jump in here, an' come hame wi' me!"' It was his turn to wet his lips, then he continued: 'An' ye's jumps in and ye's goes awa tae his hoose. An' there's a big fire, an' plenty tae eat, an' plenty tae drink. Then he says: "It's a terrible night – ye canna gae hame the night. Ye need a bed – ye must ha' yin o' mine. There is only yin, but ye shall share that wi' me." That,' he concluded, draining the bottle, 'is Glasgae hospitality.'

My companion of the night carefully screwed the cap back on the empty bottle, replaced it deep in his pocket and got astride his machine.

'Well, that's marvellous,' I said, slapping him cordially across the shoulders. 'And that actually happened to you?'

He kick-started the engine which sputtered into life again, tucked his greatcoat round his knees, then sat back on the seat and, for a moment, stared contemplatively at the handlebars. Then he admitted, 'No. Well, no – it hasna' actually happened tae me.' But suddenly, his eyes lit up through the gap in his balaclava and he said: 'But it happens tae ma sister, several nights a week!'

Then with a rev, a wave and a 'Cheerio, the noo!' he sped off, down the shimmering tram-lines; and, suitably mellowed by the unexpected nightcap, I whistled my way back to the digs, thinking what a grand place Glasgow was for a student.

However, 'yin o' Clarry's' was not a 'bed for the night', but a set of Ministry-approved protective clothing, comprising waders, mac and sou'wester. And when 'accoutred up', as they say, I looked just like the Sardine Skipper's mate.

Clarry, now with another, even larger clip-board, first led me amongst the Hereford heifers, which were quartered in tubular steel pens within the spacious barn.

Grouped in fours and fives, they were well bedded and adequately supplied with food and water and in general appearance appeared content and in good condition. Each one sported a narrow plastic collar, buckled at the bottom, which carried an identification number on either side. Some were blue, some red and some green, depending upon the final destination in Finland. This rather gaudy neckwear, set against the rich red colour of their thick coats, gave quite a gay atmosphere to the assembly, enhancing the femininity of the heifers who, for the most part, seemed very proud of their adornments.

Clarry walked amongst them importantly, calling out the breeders of the various groups as in a roll-call. The response was quite fascinating, inquisitive heads rising in apparent recognition, as the names were called.

'Jones – Penatok!' 'Lewis – The Haven!' 'Moore-

Shucknall!' 'Powell – Glan Nant!' Howell Powell's bunch had been dozing in the deep, golden straw, obviously enjoying the unaccustomed luxury of such excesses, which were not permitted back home. They got up one by one and stretched lazily, in recognition of the announcement of their presence, and I was proud to see that their coats carried a bloom as rich and silky as any there. No trace now of the yellow tint of copper deficiency.

'If ye see anything ye don't like,' said Clarry, peering over the top of his specs, 'speak up. There are a few with running eyes and one or two tender on their feet, but that could be from the change of grub,' he added. 'And there's one flighty bitch, that tried to jump the rails. But apart from that – all's well.'

'The final check is due on Tuesday morning,' I confirmed. He nodded, then changed direction, saying, 'Now for the gents!'

Leaving the long barn, we crossed to another half-covered yard, at the back of which stood a row of new loose-boxes, each with their half-doors closed and held by strong bolts, with a flat iron bar across the width of each, for extra security.

'Four bulls,' declared Clarry, consulting his board. 'Thomas's Benbow; Payne's Lucky Chance – they're reserves. And Griffiths' Windy and Paxton's Donhill Porchester – both to go. Reserves first!' He stepped forward and unbolted the top of the nearest door.

'Benbow!' he announced.

Benbow was two years old and lay with his back towards us. Slowly he turned his head and peered upwards, blinked a few times, then turned away.

'Don't think he likes being a reserve,' said Clarry. 'Never mind, laddie,' he consoled. 'Many are called, but few are chosen – it's the same in the Ministry of Agriculture.'

In the adjoining box was Lucky Chance – he was younger and smaller, but a compact little bull who already had the 'scaffolding' up. Given another twelve months he would be a really fine animal. Lucky was more interested in our presence than Benbow and immediately came up to the door to sniff at my mackintosh sleeve. 'He's the friendliest of the lot,' remarked Clarry, scratching the bull's curly forehead.

'Knew his father,' I said and briefly told Clarry about the caesarian.

'Pity ye canna take him instead of one of these two,' he commented, closing the door and moving along the boxes, 'Windy's no so bad, he's only a yearling like Lucky. But that Donhill Porchester – now there's a different kettle of fish aw'together. Got a bit of old man Paxton in him, I shouldnae' wonder.'

He showed me Windy, who huffed and puffed a bit, but without any intended aggression – and then we proceeded to the last box.

'I'll just open the door a wee bit first. He disna' care for sudden intrusions,' explained Clarry, as he cautiously drew the bolts, which were well oiled and slid quietly back; then he gently eased the top section ajar. As the gap widened, I peered over his shoulder to spy Donhill Porchester's great square rump, with a tail as thick as a tree trunk suspended from it. Beyond, his heaving girth led into powerful shoulders, running forward to form the mountainous crest of his neck, disappearing downwards. His head was out of sight.

'He'll do his war dance in a minute,' said Clarry. 'Just ye's wait.'

However, Donhill Porchester did not move for several seconds; then, with a snort from his still invisible nostrils, that sounded like a gigantic steam engine starting up, he flicked his nearside foreleg backwards, propelling a great clod of bedding directly at us.

Clarry got it full in the face, though I was more fortunate and just collected the fringes of the soggy mass.

'Ye evil monster!' spluttered Clarry. 'I hope ye drown in the Baltic Sea!' Then he cleared his eyes and face, qualifying his outburst by turning to me and adding: 'Just him, ye know. Just him.'

Before I could become too concerned about the implications of Clarry's volatile remarks, the great bull turned about, his massive head now filling the aperture. For a two-year-old, he was magnificent – no wonder Paxton had been so keen for him to go, for his physique was certainly something of which any breeder would be proud; he would undoubtedly be held in the highest esteem for producing such a champion, both at home and abroad. An accolade that, I knew, Paxton would dearly love to receive.

Broad of head, eyes bold and well set apart, Donhill Porchester had an intelligent look and, to my mind, in no way malicious – rather more mischievous. His horns were well balanced, evenly curved and fine-pointed and in sharp contrast to the large brass ring in his nose, which I had inserted some time previously.

'You're a mean old devil, so y'are!' shouted Clarry, raising his clip-board as he spoke.

'He's just playful,' I said, hopefully – for indeed, I had never seen him quite so truculent before. But scarcely had the words left my lips, than the great hulk took one pace backwards, lowered his head and drove it at the door, like a Churchill tank.

It was a good job that the woodwork was sound, for the force of his assault made the timbers groan and the iron bar strain, as it held them in place.

'Playful, eh?' gasped Clarry, recoiling from the onslaught. His sou'wester was now completely askew. 'Playful! Well, laddie, whatever bliddy games you're goin' tae play together – count me oot!'

We closed the half-door swiftly, in case he decided to try for a clearance, then repaired to Clarry's hut. He made some tea and laced it generously with Bell's. 'A wee drap of internal antiseptic', as he termed it – and a gesture for which I was very grateful.

Donhill Porchester was going to be a handful and no mistake – but it was no good complaining. Perhaps he would settle down once we were on the move – on the other hand, he might grow even more fractious. It was going to be a risky business.

*　*　*

Whilst the daily rounds had still to be seen to and an effort made to get as many outstanding jobs as possible completed before I left, there was still plenty of time to imagine some horrific situations that might occur during the voyage. Mass outbreaks of pneumonia or 'blackleg', for instance – the latter a rapid killer of recently housed cattle in exceptionally humid conditions. Then there could be abortions, broken limbs or my worst fear – one tonne of mad bull rampaging about the decks, completely out of control.

Bob Hacker could not help much when it came to medical requirements, for he had only accompanied small groups, whereas drugs for over eighty cattle were of a different order.

I finally decided that I would limit my medical aids to what I could get into my case – or the late G. R. Hacker's case, to be precise – which was accompanying me in the hope that the old vet's spirit would come along as well, for I was sure to need some support. Bob Hacker had said that when I was in trouble, his father would open the right drawers for me, and, with that comforting thought in mind, I put pessimism behind and settled down to consider seriously what problems could arise.

I narrowed it down to the three 'C's': namely: catarrh, conjunctivitis and constipation.

The first two complaints might well result from crowded conditions, especially if the ventilation was not adequate and the holds battened down – dust and humidity being two potent factors in pneumonia problems. I therefore packed some bottles of penicillin and streptomycin and eye ointments, in the event of the dust causing conjunctivitis. Stomach disorders and constipation due to the dietary change and unusual motion, I hoped to combat with some 'nux vomica' powders and a half hundredweight of

Epsom Salts – which, I thought, should at least shift something. The latter requirement forced me to depart from my original intention of taking only what I could carry in the medical bag.

As for Donhill Porchester, I packed sedative injections, a general surgical pack, local anaesthetic, wound dressing, several bandages and a large roll of hospital cotton-wool – hoping, secretly, that I should have no use for any of it, either for the heifers and bulls or – equally importantly – for myself!

While my attentions were for the most part taken up with the health and comforts of the cattle that were to be in my care, Diana was even more concerned about my safety and personal well-being during the voyage. Since we had married, I left all my sartorial arrangements to her, but what to wear on a cattle boat was not the sort of thing she normally had to decide upon. Had the Ministry of Agriculture had their way, I should no doubt have been attired in the 'Skipper Sardine' outfit for the duration of the trip; however, their jurisdiction did not extend that far.

So I decided to take some old shirts and trousers that could be disposed of on completion of the trip, together with a thin waterproof suit that could be disinfected and used for the more formal cattle occasions on landing. Seasickness pills, Mars bars, notebook, indigestion tablets – nothing was forgotten that would ease a sailor's passage over the foreign seas.

Mcbean's contribution was rather unusual and, in a way, a preparation for things to come. He lent me a book containing excerpts from the diary of one Thomas Aston, a butcher from Monmouth, who emigrated with his family to America in 1852, sailing from Bristol. On my last Saturday night ashore I felt quite unsettled, so, before going to bed, I read for a while.

It was a fascinating record. Mr Aston, so it told, took seven head of thoroughbred Hereford cattle, fourteen Cotswold sheep, two shepherd dogs and over two tons of luggage, having had the ship *Mary Ann* especially partitioned off for his family. Seven weeks and three days it took to cross, and the stock of cattle fodder was so low that they were finally fed on sea biscuits soaked in cold water. Neither were they without their losses:

*Tuesday April 20th*
The wind changed to westward, blowing very hard with rain. Night brought a heavy gale. Waves rolling heavily and tossing all our boxes and packages over one another and knocking our poor beasts about the deck in a dreadful manner. One of the cows was dead in the morning and the other cow almost dead. Was obliged to kill her. The others were very much bruised.

*Tuesday April 27th*
Rain. Wind blowing southward and a rough sea. Passed a boat bound for England. I killed a sheep and sold part of it to the passengers.

*Friday April 30th*
Wind changed again to southwest. The steward's mate robbed the cabin of some money, for which he received a dozen lashes and the captain made him parade the deck with 'thief' written upon his back for punishment.

*Sunday May 9th*
Fine and calmer. Held prayer meeting. Mr Goslin read the prayers and Mr Williams and we, answered him.

*Saturday May 15th*
We made the sailors a jolly good plum pudding for their dinner, for their good conduct. Messrs Williams, Goslin, Humphries and myself found the ingredients between us, for which they were very thankful.

*Wednesday May 19th*
We witnessed a funeral at sea. A child about twelve

months belonging to a man of the name of Morgan from Langarsen, died on the night before. It had been ill some time. Put it in a coffin with something to sink it, the captain reading the burial service.

*Tuesday June 1st*
Fine and clear. Saw several porpoises and seven dolphins. At eleven o'clock we harpooned a fine porpoise.

*Wednesday June 2nd*
Very fine, too. Cut up the porpoise early. We all tried some for our breakfasts. A great part of the fish is very much like a pig only handsomer. It was very fat. About mid-day the wind blew very hard, which made us all ill. Went to bed without any supper.

They docked on Saturday the fifth of June, 1852, in New York harbour, after losing one more heifer. 'As handsome a place as I ever saw,' wrote Thomas Aston in conclusion – and after seven weeks and three days at sea, I didn't wonder.

Over one hundred years ago, those Herefords sailed the Atlantic and, as a breed, they had crossed the high seas in all directions ever since, taking their productivity, vigour and fertility to enhance beef production throughout the world.

And now I was to have a hand in it, too. Perhaps not in such a dramatic fashion as Mr Aston on the *Mary Ann*, with his prayers and porpoises, but in some way, his experiences had made me feel differently about the whole trip; despite my initial forebodings, I was really looking forward to it.

★   ★   ★

I had finished routine work on Saturday at lunchtime and had been given the rest of the weekend and the following

Monday to prepare. So I was a trifle annoyed when the phone rang at seven o'clock on the Sunday morning, when I was supposed to be off duty. But the caller soon brought me to my senses: it was Clarry, with some most disturbing news.

'That damned Donhill Porchester has broken out in the night, an' smashed the place tae bits,' he gasped. 'Gone on the rampage like a mad thing. Flattened two wheelbarrows and a pressure cleaner in the alley, ripped open about twenty bags of feed, bent two gates and put a bliddy great hole in the side of my office!'

'Have you caught him?' I asked.

'Aye. Well, once he'd finished, he seemed quiet enough, an' we got him back into another box.'

'What on earth got into him, Clarry?'

'Damned if I know! A brainstorm, I shouldnae' wonder – if he's got a brain! He's a menace, Hugh – ye canna' trust him. If you want my opinion, he's too risky tae take. But then, that's your decision. If it was me, though, I'd send him back tae Paxton – they make a fine pair!'

Refuse to take him! What a thought! Paxton would have my guts for garters if I did that. He'd take it as a personal insult – no way would he accept that his bull was unmanageable.

Of course, it had to happen: 'sod's Law' – it could not have been anyone else's bull. Though it should not matter whose bull it was: my decision ought not to be swayed, just because it belonged to a client. Then I remembered the Finn with the steely eyes, saying: 'We wish them to be of good temperament – no wild animals, please.' And I, sticking my neck out again, with, 'Good temperament is something for which Herefords are renowned.'

Well, if that bull was going to jeopardise the shipment with his madness – Paxton or no – he was not going!

'I'll come straight down, Clarry,' I said, 'and I'd better let Ernie Shelton know as well.'

'That's not all, either,' said Clarry, with a sigh. 'He upset all the other bulls with his antics and Windy's been sweating and blowing hard ever since; he looks as if he could be starting pneumonia.'

'Thank goodness we've got reserves,' I said. 'I'll be with you shortly.' And, ringing off, I re-dialled and got in touch with Ernie.

Surprisingly enough, he did not seem overdisturbed, probably because he was already well versed in the unpredictabilities of cattle exports. Together with the fact that, once again, the buck was gently passed when he concluded: 'Well, Hugh, now's the time to make your mind up. Mad bulls and dead bulls are no good on the other side.'

Arranging to meet him at Worlton, I put the phone down and lay back.

Diana, who had been listening in silence, sat up on one elbow. 'What's wrong?' she asked.

'That Donhill Porchester's gone berserk,' I replied, staring at the ceiling.

'What will happen, Hugh?' Di put her arm on my shoulder.

'He may not be going.'

'Poor Mr Paxton,' she said. 'I expect he'll be disappointed.'

'Yes,' I said, visualising the scene. 'He probably will!'

The trail of destruction made the quarantine station appear as if a whirlwind had struck. The place was littered with broken hay bales, ruptured meal bags, compressed wheelbarrows and an amount of damage more consistent with a herd stampede than with one bull – even one of his proportions.

'I think he got into one pen of heifers,' said Clarry, who was tacking some paper bags over the gaping hole in the side of his wooden shed. 'At least, the top rail is bent – but they seem aw'right.'

'Let's have a look at the cause of the trouble,' I said, and Clarry led off to the back of the buildings, where an isolated bull box was situated.

'Should have had him in here from the start,' he grunted and opened the wooden door to reveal a tubular steel gate immediately behind.

'There he is, the mean old sod! Expect ye're mighty pleased with yer performance!' he shouted. 'Well, ye've probably done yersel' oot of a trip abroad. An' serve ye right!'

The culprit once again had his back to the door, but this time he did not turn round immediately, just hung his head while Clarry continued to lambast him. 'Ye'd be better in sandwiches! So ye would!' he said, irritably.

At that, Donhill Porchester did swing his great head round and glared at Clarry, as if the last remark was too much. Then he shook his shoulders, gave a snort and shuffled the rest of his great body around to face us.

It was difficult to see why he had got into such a rage, for now he appeared calm enough, and although he did not seem to take too kindly to Clarry, his eye was never wild or angry as one might expect with a genuinely evil bull. In fact, to look at him at that moment, one could hardly say he was too risky to take. But could I trust him not to let the side down in the future? Turning him down, because he was too dangerous to travel, would be difficult enough to explain to Paxton – but even more, it would be a sad reflection on the Hereford breed, which I was still convinced was one of the most manageable and trustworty of them all.

On top of this, Windy was running a temperature and blowing like a grampus. The commotion had definitely upset him, maybe because he had wanted to join in the fun and could not! I commenced treatment with antibiotics – but unless the response was dramatic, he was going to be a non-starter as well.

Ernie Shelton did show concern when he arrived and found that Windy was causing problems, too.

'I know we've got reserves,' he said, drumming his fingers on the table in Clarry's bull-battered shed, 'but losing both "first choice" bulls is bad. Not the thing to impress the buyers – not the thing.'

'S'pose yer could give that maniac a bit of a sleeper,' suggested Clarry. 'But when it wears off – will he do it again?'

'I don't think he's ever been like this before,' I said. 'As far as I know, anyway. Bob Hacker did say he got a bit "waspy" at the Ministry Test. Yet when I punched a hole in his nose for that ring, he was very reasonable. And if anything should have made him mad, that should.'

'Well, Hugh!' said Ernie. 'You're the expert. Whatever you say, we'll abide by.'

'You're the expert!' There it was again – that backhanded compliment, that really meant, 'You carry the can!'

'When do I have to decide?' I asked.

'Final check, day after tomorrow,' said Ernie. 'You can chuck out anything you don't like then.'

'I'll need to see Windy again tomorrow, anyway. So we'll give him until then,' I suggested.

Ernie agreed and, after looking at one of the heifers that had developed a lameness and signing Clarry's book, I drove back to Ledingford with quite a bit on my mind.

How, for instance, could one be expected to predict an animal's behaviour? Even when I was young, I had learnt how difficult that was – through Boggy, my much loved cat, when I once took a baby rabbit from him, that he had caught in the Trevethin Wood. Boggy's look of hostility and anger at me for taking away his trophy, made me realise that natural animal instincts over-ride any element of loyalty or companionship, when they are put to the test. How was I to know if Paxton's bull would do this again? It was anybody's guess.

Had he done it before? Now there was a point – had he done it before? There was one man who should know better than anybody. Not Paxton, but Mason, his stockman. I always got on well with Mason, so when I got home, I decided to give him a ring.

I could not get hold of him until he came in for tea at five o'clock. I explained the situation to him and the problem I was having about taking Donhill Porchester.

'If he sets a bad example, apart from being dangerous, the exports could suffer in the future. This first consignment has got to be as near perfect as possible,' I told him, 'or they'll be taking Angus or some other beef breed instead.'

'Sorry 'e's given you so much trouble, Mr Lasgarn,' apologised Mason, in his slow Hereford drawl. 'Can't understand 'im. I mean ter say, you knows 'ow good 'e was when you put that ring in 'im. Not many bulls would stand for it like that.'

'Bob Hacker said he played up at the Test,' I reminded him.

'Ah well!' said Mason. 'That were a Ministry job – an 'e don' like them black macs an' disinfectant, don' matter whose wearin' 'em. Could be the Pope 'imself, but if 'e 'ad a black mac on an' smelled of carbolic – e'd get the same.'

'Now why does that upset him?' I asked, beginning to see a glimmer of light.

'Ever since the Ministry Livestock Officer came to pass 'im for service, an' pulled on 'is balls a bit 'ard. 'E 'ad a black mac on.'

That, I thought, was a fair enough reason and, indeed, I was beginning to see Donhill Porchester's point of view as far as the Ministry of Agriculture was concerned, bearing in mind that Clarry's attitude, in itself, was quite provoking. 'I can understand that,' I agreed. 'But it doesn't account for him breaking out at night and smashing the place up.'

'No', said Mason, thoughtfully. Then, after a slight pause, he added: 'Don' suppose you got a heifer bullin', down there? 'E likes the ladies, an' if there was summat in the wind – boy, 'e'd take a bit of stoppin'.'

'Impossible,' I said. 'They're all in calf, with veterinary certificates.'

I heard Mason give a throaty chuckle. 'Lord, so they may, Mr Lasgarn, but I'll bet 'is nose agin a vet's piece o' paper, any day.'

65

My mind ran back to the pen of heifers that he was thought to have visited – it just could be the answer.

'Thanks, Mason,' I said. 'I think you've cracked it – and saved his bacon, into the bargain.'

'There's another thing, if you don' mind me sayin',' he replied. 'But 'e don' like being called Donhill Porchester either; we just calls 'im Chester – 'e likes that much better.'

My researches completed, there was one more important thing to be done. I called up to Diana who was bathing Sara. 'I'm going to pop down to Worlton,' I shouted up the stairs.

'What for?' she called back.

'To see if Chester's nose is better than a bit of vet's paper,' I explained. 'Won't be long.'

And off I set for the quarantine station.

Clarry was in the caravan, where he slept, finishing his evening meal.

'I think I've got the answer to Chester's problem,' I told him.

'Whose problem . . .?' he spluttered, as I hauled him away from his supper.

'Bucket of hot water, soap and towel – an' I'll show you.'

'What aboot the macs an' sou'westers?' he yelled, as I made for the pen with the bent rail, to which Chester had paid his attentions.

'That, Clarry,' I shouted back, 'is part of the problem!'

The heifers were in two batches regarding pregnancy. One third were supposed to be between six and seven months in calf and the rest around three months. Their state had been confirmed and certified by each breeder's own veterinary surgeon, before entering quarantine.

I stripped off, donned my red rubber apron and, as Clarry haltered each heifer in turn, I examined them internally.

They were in the three months category, the first few being definitely in calf. My hand felt the womb, which was as large as a rugby ball at that stage and, by tapping gently

66

upon the elastic wall, I could feel the tiny foetus, bobbing like a cork beneath my fingers.

But when I came to the fifth – there was no rugby ball. Just the turgid, hosepipe-like structures of the empty uterine horns, their consistency typical of the oestrus state, which I confirmed by the presence of a follicle on the ovary.

'She's bulling!' I shouted excitedly.

'You sure?' queried Clarry.

'Bull's nose to a piece of paper, I am,' I said. 'Come on – let's go and tell Chester the good news.'

The non-pregnant heifer was excluded from the final selection. Whether a mistake had been made at the pregnancy diagnosis, or whether it was a case of foetal reabsorption, which sometimes occurred in the early stages, was impossible to tell.

However, Chester had diagnosed the condition; perhaps more exuberantly than was quite necessary, but at least he had saved us the embarrassment of taking an 'empty' heifer, which would not have helped future sales very much. Windy, however, did not make the grade, developing an acute pneumonia, as a result of which he had to be withdrawn.

This left me to choose one of the reserves and it was with a deal of pleasure that I decided Lucky Chance should get the trip.

All the heifers passed the final check and Clarry wished me 'aw' the best for the morn's day!'

# 5

'A fair wind and a full sail' – the sailor's dream – was all that I now should have been wishing. Yet there was one matter that still concerned me and I decided to attend to it that Sunday night; it would take but a few hours – and it was a trip back home to Abergranog.

To say 'back home' was unfair, because Ledingford with Di and Sara was now my home; although there is always a longing, a 'hiraeth' as they say in the valleys, that is never completely shed by any born of Wales.

The reason for my mission was, however, not to satisfy that innate yearning, but to collect a woolly hat and a pullover from my Aunt Min.

Aunt Min was a tonic to anyone feeling down in the dumps, for at the age of seventy-five, having been widowed for ten of them and bedridden for five, she still radiated an incredible cheerfulness and boundless optimism.

She was one of my few surviving relatives in the valley and, though I was able to spend little time with her, of the few precious hours that I did whenever I went back to Abergranog, I always felt rejuvenated by her spirit.

She passed the time knitting – something of which she was still eminently capable – and kept half the village supplied with gloves and scarves, and me, in particular, with woolly hats and mittens.

When I told her I was taking to the high seas, she had promised to provide a very special hat and a thick double-knit pullover to keep me warm during my Baltic adventure.

Unfortunately, she had only managed to complete the work a few days previously, far too late for posting, and someone had phoned to ask if I could collect it. Knowing how hard she had worked and how disappointed she would be if I did not use her gift, I decided to make a quick dash down to see her.

Crossing the border at Llangua, my lights panned across the newly erected sign with the Red Dragon prominently displayed. 'Croeso y Cymru,' it said – 'Welcome to Wales' – and I immediately felt the 'hiraeth' tingling in my blood once again.

For the next twenty miles, memories came flooding back – happy, sad, boisterous, reflective – and when I came to the Daren Pitch, a few miles from the village, I thought of Uncle Fred, Aunt Min's late husband and one of my boyhood heroes.

Uncle Fred was the sportsman of the family, a great rugby player; although he was never capped, he once had a trial for the Principality, which, whilst not equal to the supreme accolade, was worth many a pint in club circles.

He captained Talybran on one of the highest, windswept pitches in the country and was reputed to be able to curl a ball from inside his own half, out over Talybran Cemetery which lay alongside, and back on the prevailing wind, dead centre between the opposition posts.

'If they can't come now,' he would say of the departed, 'least we can do, is give 'em a look at the ball!'

But Talybran pitch suffered from the elements and the scruffing and scraping of some of the heftiest boots in Wales; so much so that it became denuded to the point of being unplayable, there being no tilth below, just shale and compacted coal dust.

It was decided that the pitch needed relaying, and Uncle Fred knew where he could obtain some turf – believe it or not, from a farmer in Herefordshire. So I was not the first Lasgarn by any means to cross the border, for my Uncle Fred, driving Arwen Powell's coal lorry and accompanied

69

by a goodly number of the Talybran forward line, one Saturday out of season went up-country to collect it. They took the turf – and good it was, too. Then they called at a few hostelries on the way home, to sample the 'wine' of the county.

It must have been well into the small hours when Arwen Powell's trusty Bedford struggled up the Daren Pitch with a couple of tons of Herefordshire sod and a bunch of well-away Welshmen.

At the top, near the bridge, they were stopped by the police. Sergeant Donaghue was on patrol, and he flagged down the load, just as it reached the crest.

Lorries returning from Herefordshire in the small hours were deeply suspect; in fact even in broad daylight their cargo might well conceal potatoes, swedes, apples, plums and an odd lamb or two that might have strayed onto the highway. If Herefordshire was part of the garden of England, to the Welsh a bit of 'scrumping' was more than fair game!

Sergeant Donaghue, six foot six and Irish, stood back and surveyed the load with an incredulous eye.

He walked round it twice, prodded the sheet, then turned his hand slowly in the manner of a conductor encouraging *molto largo* – except that his expression was far from musical, but rather an indication to Uncle Fred, who was driving, to wind down his window.

'Freddie Lasgarn, is it now!' he perceived, flashing his lantern into the cab. 'And what might you be doing on the Daren in such company, at this time in the morning?'

'We've been up to Hereford, Sergeant,' said Uncle Fred, quite polite and proper.

'Hereford, now. Is that so?' said Donaghue.

Uncle Fred, smiled and nodded amiably, ignoring the stifled laughter from his mates.

'And what would you be transporting under that sheet from Hereford, then, Freddie Lasgarn?' persisted the sergeant inquisitively.

'A rugby pitch,' said Uncle Fred.

'A rugby pitch!' Donaghue stood back a pace and shone his lantern on the load.

Then, burning with suspicion, he turned on Uncle Fred again.

'And what would you be doing, transporting a rugby pitch into Wales for, Freddie, me boy?'

Uncle Fred, cheeks red and eyes smiling, winked broadly.

'Talybran Rugby Club, Sergeant, an' we've been playin' away!'

I laughed to myself as I cleared the top of the Daren and put my foot down for the last few miles, when suddenly I heard the sound of bells. For a moment I was puzzled – there was no church in the vicinity – but on second thoughts, it was not that sort of bell. Then alongside drove a Wolsley police car and, pulling ahead, signalled me to stop – just a few hundred yards from where they had copped my Uncle Fred!

Two policemen got out; one shone a torch on my number plate, whilst the other, a sergeant, not quite six foot six but pretty hefty, came to my door.

I was about to get out – they always said you were at a disadvantage if someone talked down to you – but the sergeant must have been well aware of that, for he leaned on the door and I had to resort to winding down the window.

For a few seconds he just looked at me, his face devoid of the slightest expression. Then his colleague, having noted the description of my vehicle, held out his notebook for the sergeant to see.

He looked at it. Then looked at the car and then back to me.

'Good evening, sir!' he said, eventually. 'And where might you have come from?'

'Hereford,' I said, smiling at the coincidence.

'Nice to have a sense of humour, sir,' he said dryly. 'Where would you be going to, now?'

'Abergranog,' I said, this time without a smile. The sergeant nodded and looked at his mate. 'Anything wrong, officer?' I asked. Just my luck, I thought. Crashed the speed limit of all things – never thought about it.

'Your boot's open, sir,' he said. 'Thought you might lose something.'

My relief was self-evident.

'Thank goodness for that,' I said. 'You frightened the pants off me for a moment.'

'Now did I, sir?' he replied, again without a flicker of emotion.

'Yes,' I said, slightly disturbed at his coolness.

'But it won't be the first time, will it, sir?' he said. I did not understand. 'Once for you, Mr Lasgarn, and once for me. You still playing the fiddle?'

Only then did a smile rise from the corner of his lips, and as I studied his features and re-appraised the tone of his voice, another memory came flooding back – of the Park and the Shelter and my old violin.

\* \* \*

In my youthful days in Abergranog, music played a considerable part in the community and one was expected to sing in a choir, play the piano or learn some orchestral instrument.

I would have loved to play the bugle in the Boy's Brigade, or even a drum; but Mother disapproved of such organisations, saying they enticed young lads into the Army. So instead, I was 'put to the violin'.

It was an unhappy relationship from the start, despite the patient efforts of my long-suffering tutor, Mr Pearce, to obtain some semblance of co-ordination in my fingers and a degree of acceptable sound from the strings. Every Thursday, after school, I would scrape away for half an hour in the front room of Bryntyrion House, until the dear old gentleman would remove his half-moon specs, wipe his eye and say, thankfully: 'I think that's enough for today, Hugh. Quite enough.'

Then I would pack my instrument into its black wooden case, which resembled a small coffin and weighed equally heavily, and, leaving Bryntyrion, would make my way to Marshall's shop. Armed with a ration coupon and pocket money I would purchase a whipped cream walnut and repair to the Shelter in the Park, where I would sit and relish my favourite treat.

The Shelter was a small open-fronted building with bench seating around the walls; there were lavatories either side, the 'Men's' to the left and the 'Women's' to the right. From the vantage point of the Shelter, one could look down over the lawns and rose gardens, the children's playground and the roof of the Co-op slaughterhouse that adjoined the perimeter.

The Park had been left to the public by a wealthy mine master who once lived in the grounds; the house had long been demolished but the garden, which was immaculately maintained by the 'Parky', an energetic little man called Ernie Brewer, remained intact and was a welcome oasis of scent and colour amid the drab surroundings of the village.

Park sounds, too, I shall never forget: creaking swings, flushing lavs, Ernie's clattering Atco mower and kids shouting; but the most unique sound in Abergranog Park was that of the wicket gate that led up to the rose garden. Hung at an angle, it had a vicious, coiled black spring that caused it to snap shut like a rat trap, with a crack that echoed around the Park. There was a mean trick played by certain boys, of opening it for the old men who came to sit in the garden, and letting it go before they were right through. It would whip back, dislodging their specs and rosewood pipes, knocking walking sticks from their grasp.

The boys would shout: 'Sorry Dad. It slipped, mun!'

But it never did. They let it go on purpose and we all knew that they did. Yet nobody said.

Frightened of Cotter we were, or rather Cotter's gang. The Maesllwych Mafia. They were the Bosses of the Park, persecuting everyone, young and old alike. If you crossed Cotter, you were for it.

'Well, Lasgarn! What are we goin' to do with you now, boyo?'

I can hear his thin sing-song voice to this day, jeering into my ear, my face pressed hard into the wet grass by two of his henchmen.

The Mister Big of Abergranog Park.

If, in Cotter's opinion, one's actions were not too remiss, the punishment was relatively mild, like rubbing red ash from the pathway into your hair; sterner retribution took the form of either Cotter himself or one of his mates peeing in your pocket or your cap.

But if really severe measures were warranted, Cotter could devise those, too. A favourite of his was to frog-march you down to the Co-op slaughterhouse and push you over the low wall into the offal alley, where you trampled the guts until a slaughterman heard your cries and opened the road gate. He would invariably curse you and threaten to tell your parents, who would know anyway; for even if you risked going back through the Park to wash your boots and socks in the ornamental fish pool, the smell would still hang on.

For me, though, the punishment that started it all was when they caught me eating my whipped cream walnut in the Shelter after a violin lesson. I was happily savouring my delight, when who should come swaggering out of the 'Men's' but Cotter and his spotty sidekick, Dorny Longbotham.

The Longbothams kept a shop on the Garn and pronounced their name 'Longbowtham', but everyone else called them 'Longbottom'.

Dorny, or 'our Donald' to his Mam, had suffered many jibes over his unfortunate surname until Cotter took him over, but having been elected to the hierarchy of the Gang, no one dared take it in vain any more.

'Eatin', Lasgarn?' Cotter observed, in a surprisingly amiable tone. 'Now there's nice for 'ew!' He came and sat alongside me on the bench. 'Dorny an' me likes chocolate. Don' we Dorny?'

Dorny Longbotham raised his spotty cheeks, his eyes squinting in a mean grin.

''Ow about a little share for us, then?' he whined. 'We'em very 'ungry.'

What happened next was a tragedy, for although I could make a whipped cream walnut last twenty minutes under normal circumstances, in two bites I devoured the lot, leaving just the nut, which I had saved until last, resting on top of my violin case.

Cotter's attitude changed immediately and he stood up, glowering at me as I nervously chomped on the remains of the delicacy.

'Now that was greedy, Lasgarn,' he said, slowly and deliberately. 'Very greedy indeed.'

'There's a nut on his box!' blurted Dorny, reaching towards it; but my hand beat him to the draw. Yet, as I grabbed it, Cotter kicked my feet from under me and, when I dropped my nut, he ground it into the floor with his heavy boots.

'It's a fiddle box,' said Dorny, now concentrating on my case. 'Play us a tune, then!'

'Keep your hands off that, Longbottom!' I shouted. 'An' out of my way. I'm going home!'

It was a vain attempt to sound unafraid, but my lip quivered, giving the show away, and Cotter saw it.

'Heared what 'e called 'ew, Dorny?' said Cotter, imitating surprise. 'Dorny don' like people callin' 'im that. Do 'ew, Dorny? 'Ew knows 'is name, Lasgarn, an' we'll 'ave to learn 'ew to say it proper. Won't we, Dorny?'

Cotter had made his move. He now had justification for any action he might care to take. Clever was Cotter in that respect, always allowing the unwitting victim to appear to have engineered the provocation.

'Well, Lasgarn,' he said again in a falsely amiable tone. 'What can we do with 'ew now, boyo?'

Dorny whispered something in his ear and grinned, and

Cotter nodded his head slowly.

As they came forward, I made a frantic dive between them, but they stopped me dead, like a pig in an alley, and dragged me into the 'Men's'.

I'd never been in the 'Men's' before.

I'd done it behind the Shelter, in the rose garden, up against Ernie's tool shed and once, with Wendel Weekes, we did it over the offal pit on top of the dead guts.

But I'd never done it in the 'Men's' proper – though I had always wanted to.

Yet the way I was dragged bodily around the partition and thrown upon the floor gave me no chance to appreciate the finer points of the convenience.

The aroma of disinfectant tingling in my nostrils and the sizzling of water filling the tanks above, were the only sensations I appreciated, other than the weight of Dorny on my back.

But the next sensation gave me a clue to what they were about, for a cold draught ran up my legs and the wet floor kissed my buttocks.

The swines were pulling my trousers off!

I kicked and thrashed to no avail; I grunted and strained; but Dorny held me firm. In fact, my antics even nelped my attackers to achieve their objective and, as I turned my head, I saw Cotter holding up my grey short trousers triumphantly.

''Oose got a longbottom now, Lasgarn? An' a wet 'un, too! Hold on, Dorny, an' I'll see if they be empty!'

I thought he was going to search my pockets, but his lumpy boots tramped past my head and he went outside.

'Piles 'ew'll be gettin', Lasgarn. Sitting on a wet floor,' said Dorny with glee.

That frightened me more than anything. I'd heard Mr Morris Ty-Gwyn talking about his in the Post Office and the agony he was in. The very thought of getting piles sickened me.

'Clear it is, mun.' Cotter was back in the 'Men's' again. 'Up with 'im, Dorny, an' quick!'

Dorny eased his weight.

'This way, "mochyn brwnt"!' Cotter commanded, and led me out by the ear.

The fact that he had called me a 'dirty pig' did not upset me, for I felt my release was imminent; but to my absolute horror they walked me across the front of the Shelter into the 'Women's', pushed me into a cubicle and slammed the door shut.

My hand grabbed at the bolt as it slid across.

'Cotter! Let me out!' I demanded.

'Don' worry, "mochyn". We'll tell Parky 'ew be 'ere!'

They laughed meanly.

'Where's my trousers?' I yelled.

'In the "Men's" bog!'

'Down the "Men's" bog!' Dorny chortled.

'Aw, Cotter! Come on, mun!'

But my pleas were useless. They left, sniggering to themselves, and I sat down in absolute despair on the fixed wooden rim of the lavatory seat.

Locked in the 'Women's' without my trousers! It was the End of the World.

I began to shiver, when suddenly I remembered my violin – funny thing to remember in a lav, but I did – Cotter would have that, too, if I did not get out. I tried the bolt again, but it was firm, jammed from the outside by some devious means.

Then I had it. I would squeeze under the partition into the adjoining cubicle and make my escape.

I was halfway under when I heard the sound of someone approaching.

My heart leaped.

Caught in the 'Women's'! Jesus! How wicked!

The shuffling footsteps were accompanied by vague mumblings, and when I heard the clatter of something falling on the floor, I knew who it was.

Not Ernie the Parky, but Maggie Cobbler.

Poor old Maggie was odd and wandered the village, talking to herself, collecting windfall wood and doing no one any harm. But Maggie was a woman and more entitled to be there than I was.

As she pushed open the cubicle door I scrabbled backwards once more into my prison.

There followed some of the most embarrassing moments of my life as I sat there, trouserless, listening to Maggie relieving herself next door.

I shut my eyes and tried to plug my ears and nose all in one go.

I don't think Maggie can have been for a week and, to cap it all, she lit her pipe and filled the whole lavatory with a grey fog. I had a terrible job to avoid coughing and nearly choked myself.

It was ages before she packed herself together again, but eventually she did and picked up her sticks and left.

It was only then that I was able to make good my escape and emerged into the cold afternoon air, sick and shaken.

I was heartened to find my violin intact. My trousers were down the pan in the 'Men's', like they had said, but despite the legs being wet, I soon regained my propriety and scanned the Park for my two assailants. They were nowhere to be seen, yet I sensed they were spying on me.

Picking up the case I made for the far gate. I knew what they would be thinking and I was determined to prove them wrong.

I would *not* tell my mother!

Neither did I, and, as I lay in bed that night, despite the ambush, I felt rather pleased with myself.

After all, although it had brought tears to my eyes, I had not actually cried; I had not lost my violin or my whipped cream walnut, apart from the nut; and, what was more, I had achieved one of my dearest ambitions – I had at last been in the 'Men's'

And as if that was not enough, I had the incredible claim of having been where few men had gone before – into the 'Women's' as well!

I could not wait for morning, to tell Wendel Weekes.

Wendel Weekes was a great pal of mine. He lived with

his parents and his elder sister, Megan, in Pegler's Row, and his Dad drove a bus for Western Welsh and bred champion Wire-Haired Terriers.

Wendel listened in admiration to my escapade, in which I gave myself a rather more heroic role than I had actually played. He was greatly impressed with my entry into the 'Men's', but thought going into the 'Women's' rather rude.

'Anytime 'ew want's to go, Wendel, I'll take 'ew in,' I informed him grandly.

'Let's go now!' said Wendel.

So go we did.

But such was his excitement that he did not make it!

We used the 'Men's' a lot after that, often quite unnecessarily.

Then, one day when we were standing outside after a somewhat wasted journey, Wendel said:

'Take us in the African Hut, Hugh.'

I suppose the request was inevitable, for I was now a bit of an adventurer in Wendel's eyes and the African Hut was the only other place in the Park we had never been in.

It was situated beneath a large willow at the end of the rose garden, an unusual circular structure made of black wood; there were two tiny windows, a low door at the front and a conical roof of straw – in fact, although it had originally been designed as a summerhouse, it had a distinctly tribal appearance, hence its name.

During the day, the old men of the village sat within, swapping memories, smoking pipes and spitting and choking in the acrid fumes that oozed eerily through the doorway and even the straw roof.

To us boys it was a rather mysterious, even sinister place, for the interior was always dark and forbidding and we rarely went near it.

However, not wishing to lose my newly acquired status, I made an immediate decision.

'We'll go tonight when the Park is closed,' I announced. 'There'll be no old men about.'

'When it's closed!' Wendel was taken aback by my bravado.

So was I. But needs must when you're a hero.

We scaled the iron gates at dusk.

All was silent.

The swings were chained, the Atco mower tucked away in its shed and the 'Men's' locked.

Easing our way through the wicket gate, Wendel and I crept stealthily towards the round-shouldered willow and the Hut beneath.

There was no smoke, but the interior was still masked by the gloom of the evening.

'It's spooky, mun,' said Wendel nervously.

'Not scared, are 'ew?' I scorned.

'Too true I am, boyo,' came the shaky reply.

'We'll go together,' I suggested. 'Do it quick. Run in. Run around. Run out!'

Taking deep breaths, we counted three and sprang for the opening – but sad to tell, my nerve failed and I stopped. Leaving little Wendel to fly through the aperture alone.

The scream came almost immediately, high-pitched and frantic. There followed a great crashing noise and, as I stepped forwards, two bodies launched at me from the Hut, knocking me backwards. I heard someone say wicked words and was conscious of the crunch of gravel and running footsteps.

It was some seconds before my head cleared, and when I did eventually recover I was confronted by Wendel standing in the doorway.

He appeared completely unscathed.

'Spooks, Wendel?' It was my voice that was shaking now.

'Spooks? No, boyo!' He grinned. 'It was Cotter and our Meg!'

'What's that 'ew got?' I eyed the bundle he was holding.

'Trousers, boyo!' Wendel held his trophy aloft. 'Cotter's!'

It was unbelievable.

'What we goin' to do now, Lasgarn?' said Wendel, imitating Cotter's whining tone.

I brushed the gravel from my jersey and straightened up, a warm glow spreading through my body as I contemplated the future.

'I think, Wendel bach...' I savoured every word. 'I think we'll come back tomorrow – when the 'Men's' is open. Cotter can manage without 'em till then!'

And here he was again, three stripes and a whistle, leaning on my car door.

'Sergeant Cotter!'

He nodded.

'What we goin' to do with 'ew now, Lasgarn?' I could have expected it, but he didn't say it.

'No, I don't play the fiddle,' I said.

'Pity,' he replied. 'You could have given us a tune. I'll shut your boot for you – wouldn't want you to drop anything else in Abergranog, would we, Mr Lasgarn?'

More than relieved, I thanked him and was about to get out, but he offered to shut it for me.

'Give my regards to your aunty!' he called, then stepped back and waved me on.

I did just that when I got to her place and she told me how Cotter was now a highly respected pillar of the community and a good copper, and in fact he had married Meg, Wendel's sister – she of the African Hut.

I drove back to Ledingford at a steady pace that night, pondering on the times I had spent in the Land of My Fathers and wondering what new adventures lay in store for me in the Land of a Thousand Lakes.

# 6

My first sighting of the *Dagmar Hansen* took my breath away. It was early morning, and a wet early morning at that.

Ernie Shelton had brought me down from Hereford ahead of the cattle, which were due from Worlton around ten o'clock. Ernie's Austin saloon juddered and jerked over the potholed surface, weaving an erratic pattern through the maze of wagon rails and gantries.

'Oh, aye!' the gateman had said with a chuckle, in answer to Ernie's request for directions. 'The floatin' cow-shed 'ew want, is it? Down at number five, boyo – come in last night.'

His description did not sound too complimentary and, as we lurched around the corner of a vast tin warehouse, following the sign to number '5', I caught sight of three vessels.

First in line was a large black freighter called the *Waka-tiki*, registered in Panama; the furthest away seemed to be a type of tanker, with a rather rusted, red hull, the name *Maria* painted unevenly upon the stern; and, sandwiched in between, completely dwarfed by its companions, lay a tiny grey boat with green decks and a black funnel.

'There she is,' said Ernie, braking sharply. 'Your transport over the briny. Neat, isn't she?'

Neat! I swallowed hard, as my memory returned to the pictures on the wall in Ernie Shelton's office, back at Ledingford. Those magnificent craft with such smooth lines, ploughing majestically through blue seas, the sun gleaming upon them from the heavens. And what had I got? A tiny little tub that would be lost in Langorse Lake – I had not expected the *Queen Elizabeth*, but what I saw before me seemed ridiculous.

'God! She's small!' I said. 'They'll never all get on that!'

'You'd be surprised,' said Ernie, as we juddered off again. 'Very economical where stowage is concerned, no wasted space on a cattle boat, Hugh.'

Indeed, I hoped I *was* going to be surprised and that Ernie's observation was correct. Granted, the size of the other vessels accentuated *Dagmar*'s minuteness, but she was certainly no more than fifty yards from stem to stern and about ten wide; and as we approached, she seemed to get even smaller – or more economical, as Ernie might put it!

I got out of the car, took a few paces back and surveyed my abode for the coming days.

To be fair, she was in good trim – 'neat' was a reasonable description.

The quarter deck, containing the cabins, was fronted by a wide-windowed bridge, carrying at each fore-corner what appeared to be two large drain-pipes rising skywards.

These rather disproportionate structures, I later learned, were part of the ventilation system, operating from the hold where the cattle were housed.

A squat black funnel, with blue rings edged in white, was tucked neatly into the rear of the raised structures. The main deck, railed at each side, was sparkling fresh, the metalwork recently painted: rails and stanchions in white, the floor green – a colour scheme, no doubt, designed to remind the stock of pastures green and hopefully encourage any reluctant bovine traveller to board more readily.

Amidships lay the hatches, incorporating a descending chute which gave access to the cattle hold. Between this and the fo'castle rose a mast, supporting a deck light and radio aerial, and flying a small, slightly crumpled Union Jack – a courtesy to her port of call.

The prow was quite graceful, rising well above the main

deck with the lettering *Dagmar Hansen* in black, upon the side.

There was no activity visible aboard. The crew, I assumed, like the little ship, were taking a rest after crossing the Irish Sea.

Yes, I decided, 'neat', was a fair description.

'Ah! The fodder!' said Ernie, pointing down the dock, and we walked over to examine it.

The bales were stacked in a tidy pile, sheeted with a tarpaulin; I dug deeply into one of them, pulled out a handful of hay from the centre and took a sniff.

'Sweet enough,' I said. 'Not too dusty.'

Ernie, who was making a rough count of the load, nodded. 'Seems okay,' he said, finally, 'Broad bran's correct and there looks like enough Epsom Salts to clean out the Bristol Channel!'

He drew his pipe from a side pocket; it was the first time he had resorted to it, a restraint for which I was thankful; the combination of Ernie's tobacco and the motion of his car, could well have given my stomach an extremely unwelcome rehearsal for the voyage ahead.

'Well, that's one worry over,' he commented, lighting up with a degree of satisfaction proportionate to the moment. 'Hell of a job if they serve up rubbish at this stage.' He blew out a cloud of smoke and gazed about. 'Damned agent should have been here by now. I think I'll take a run back up to the gate. You'd better get aboard and find your way around – see whether they've got a hammock for you.' He gave a roguish wink, jammed the pipe firmly into the corner of his mouth, got into his car and splashed noisily away.

I stood for a few seconds in the soft drizzle, contemplating my surroundings.

As a Welshman, I did have some nautical inclinations – after all, on a clear day you could see the Bristol Channel from rising ground at the back of my Aunt Min's house in Abergranog, even though it was thirty miles away.

So, throwing off my rural image and adopting a more

swashbuckling attitude, I swaggered up the gangplank in best nautical style, whistled a few notes to pipe myself aboard and dropped onto the grass-green deck of the good ship *Dagmar Hansen*.

Whether it was because she was tied up and just an extension of the jetty, or because there was neither sight nor sound of any life aboard, I found my entry into the world of ships a slight anticlimax. So, skirting the aft hatch, I made for an oak door below the bridge.

Despite the lack of human presence, I could see from the amply strawed cattle pens, viewable through the open hatch, that work was well in hand and the facilities already prepared for the cattle.

The doorway was oak-built and sturdy, with a handle not unlike that found on oldfashioned car doors; it was let into the bulkhead in such a way that a step of over a foot was required to gain entry – a feature not necessarily intended to rupture the incomer, but to prevent any wash from the deck running inside.

Tentatively, I turned the handle, side-hopped the barrier and found myself in a narrow passageway.

To my right, another closed door leading to a cabin; to my left, a small dining area with a narrow table, bench seat and chairs to seat six. The table was laid, presumably for breakfast, with thick white crockery; plates of assorted breads, some of it very black; cooked meats and sausage; a tray with cheese and a bowl of fruit.

It all looked very appetising and reassuring, for although I had thoroughly organised the cattle's requirements, I had not contemplated my own nutritional needs.

To be surprised at finding the eating arrangements so civilised rather exposed my ignorance of life at sea where, in the majority of cases, the standard of food is classed as an item of supreme importance. The days of Cap'n Bligh, pemmican, ship's biscuits and one ladle of water each, are thankfully long gone.

The passage ahead divided: on the right, leading to a companionway aloft, and on the left, to a further narrow avenue of doors. I was momentarily uncertain which direction to take, when my nostrils detected a most delectable and inviting aroma – someone was making coffee.

The smell of good coffee always brings to mind a glorious confusion of thoughts, the depth and richness of the sensation conjuring up an aura of relaxation and good living.

Despite this heady reaction to such a delight, I had still not discovered a sure and foolproof way of making good coffee myself. Ever since my university days, I had been investigating sundry methods, grinding endless varieties of beans and using innumerable contraptions to brew, percolate or cause to be made coffee that was black, brown, ginger, bitter, tasteless, and sometimes more offensive to look at than it was to the palate! Even succumbing to adverts for 'easy-to-make', 'instant', 'genuine', 'truly fresh', 'taste-bud tickling' concoctions – my results seemed no better than that made from basic principles.

In short, I fully admitted, although I was highly partial to the brew – I could not make good coffee. In my life, only other people made good coffee, and whenever I found my nose twitching to its seductive aroma, I was immediately drawn to its source, like a man hypnotised.

That was how I met George.

With my head slightly raised to savour the gloriously welcoming aroma, I followed the coffee trail, to discover it led to a galley on the left. Inside was a single occupant with his back toward me, pouring out the elixir into an assortment of large mugs.

His attire was quite un-cook-like and simple, comprising a black beret, blue overalls and clogs.

From the beret he might have been French; from the clogs Dutch; or German from his build – square head, no neck, oblong body and large feet, probably clog size eleven!

I coughed to announce my presence, but he did not hear and just kept pouring.

'Excuse me . . .'

The stocky little man jumped like a startled rabbit and, for some peculiar reason, looked all over the galley before his eyes came to rest upon me. Then he swung round, holding the large enamel coffee pot which had an extra handle on the spout, like a machine gun, and pointed it squarely at me.

'I'm the vet,' I announced. 'I'm going with the cattle.'

He eyed me suspiciously, still training the steaming spout upon my navel.

'The vet,' I repeated. 'Medico *pour les vaches*!' I wished I had worked harder at school. '*Docteur pour les animaux*!' I put an imaginary stethoscope to my ears, then, raising the invisible chest piece, pretended to listen to the coffee-laden air.

It did the trick. Suddenly his eyes lit up and his chunky, stubble-covered features exploded into a broad smile.

'Doktor! Doktor for de caddle!' he said in a loud voice, thumping the heavy pot upon the work-top. Then, wiping the palm of his left hand on his overalled buttocks, he held it out.

I was forced to use my left, too – a manoeuvre which only added to the awkwardness of the situation in that confined space.

'I am George!' he announced, in a voice loud enough to waken all the sleeping sailors in Newpool Dock. 'I am for the killing and the cutting up of the caddle – for I am three years in butcher's house. I am very good man for you!' He pumped my hand vigorously, adding a considerable degree of physical exertion to his rather unnerving intro-duction.

'I hope we won't have any need for that,' I said, detach-ing my hand at last.

'Nay, nay,' said George. 'The *Dagmar*, she is the most finest boat and all will be happy, and eat and sleep like a ladies' liner.' By which I assumed he meant 'cruise'. 'Now you take coffee,' he said, proffering a mug. 'George make it. It is good – better than cook. He loco.' He growled menacingly, like a bear, and advanced towards me, hands raised like claws. 'Cook madman!' he moaned – then suddenly broke off his impersonation to convulse his stocky frame in laughter.

A butcher and a mad cook – that, I thought, was quite some start for my maiden voyage!

But the coffee was good, excellent, in fact – thick and sharp, but not bitter, and as its fragrance crept into my nostrils, despite the character of the company so far, I suddenly felt at home on little *Dagmar*.

'You have happy time with us,' said George.

'I'm sure we all will,' I replied.

'Caddle, too,' said George, beaming away.

'Caddle, too,' I confirmed, and took a further pleasing draught of the steaming brew.

The 'caddle' arrived slightly earlier than anticipated, at nine o'clock or 'O' nine hundred hours, as Ernie put it: having now donned his 'shipping' hat, he was full of quayside jargon.

Six stock wagons, five for the heifers and a separate one for the bulls, drove in convoy to the head of the jetty, with Clarry Norris riding 'shotgun'.

'All present and correct, Mr Mate!' he announced, with a mock salute.

'How's Chester?'

Clarry sucked air through the corner of his mouth. 'No verra keen, laddie,' he said. 'No verra keen. Didna' want tae leave the comforts of Worlton and the company of yours truly, d'ye see. Had to use a wee bit o' gentle persuasion.'

'You didn't upset him?' I asked, with some concern.

Clarry shook his head somewhat unconvincingly. 'Let's say he's just a mite unsettled,' he replied. 'No one of his best days.'

Chester! I knew he was going to be trouble and wondered again whether I had made the right decision in taking him.

In several ways I had gone against general opinion.

Clarry, I was sure, would gladly have certified him too dangerous to travel. Ernie Shelton was also aware of the problem and had emphasised on several occasions that I could refuse him if I so wished.

Then there was the Finn, he of the steel-grey eyes and the secret smile: 'No wild animals, please,' he had said.

'Good temperament is something for which Herefords are renowned,' I had countered.

'Then there is no problem . . .' he had said.

Now Chester was kicking off the trip by 'not having one of his best days.'

Would he have some good days at sea? I wondered.

I should be so lucky!

'Hugh!' It was Ernie. 'We're going aboard to meet the Skipper – you'd better come.'

'I'll gang alang wi' ye, too,' said Clarry. 'Might just tap a wee drap o' duty free.'

Clarry's hopes were soon realised when, after crowding into the chart room, the Captain, a heavily built man of rather piratical appearance, produced a large bottle of brandy to accompany another round of coffee.

Captain Schwarz was his name and it suited him, for his hair and prolific beard were as black as a raven's wing.

At his right hand sat his First Mate, small and dapper – Mr Mumme.

Our team consisted of Ernie who immediately, from his bottomless brief case, extracted pile after pile of forms, certificates and large brown envelopes. Then there was the agent, a rather trendy young man called Willows; MacLowell, the Divisional Veterinary Officer of Newpool, attired in regulation black mac and wellies and, from the smell, heavily steeped in Jeyes Fluid; myself and Clarry.

'A seat, gentlemen, please,' invited the Captain, in a deep rumble of accented English. 'You will all take brandy.'

It was not an invitation, rather an order. Although it was not my habit to imbibe at 'O' nine hundred hours, I was prepared to assume it was all part of nautical life and decided that I should get into the swing as soon as possible.

It did cross my mind that, as well as seeing the Bristol Channel from the back of Aunt Min's house, one could also, on a clear day, glimpse the sunlight glinting upon the windows of the giant crane cabins at Newpool Docks from Abergranog Baptist Chapel, where we had gone to learn about drinking.

Talfyn Thomas, Chief Air Raid Warden of the locality, ran the Band of Hope, and I wondered, as I reached for my glass, whether his teaching had had more effect upon my schoolboy companions of the day, Wendel Weekes and Boxy Potter. Drinking the Devil's Brew for breakfast, indeed!

On board, Ernie Shelton came into his own. He sat, facing the Captain, in a perfectly upright position, making the most of his small stature; and though, despite this physical adjustment, he was still very much dwarfed by the large German, the sharpness of his personality was in no way diminished.

'Captain,' he began, 'with your permission...' Schwarz nodded. 'May I introduce...' He went around the table: MacLowell, DVO, Newpool; Willows the agent; Clarry, who was already on his second brandy, and myself. 'Mr Hugh Lasgarn, our veterinary surgeon,' he concluded, 'will be travelling with you.'

The Captain nodded again, but made no further gesture of welcome, whilst Mumme looked at me rather coldly, then dropped his head sharply in a form of bow which, had he been standing, might well have been accompanied by the clicking of heels.

Bills of lading, derogations, certifications, banker's drafts, stock lists – all were passed before the assembled company's eyes by Ernie, and with such dexterity that one might even have suspected a sleight of hand. Especially when Ernie referred to that part of the money due to be received at loading:

'I am obliged to give you sight of this cheque,' he said,

flashing it briefly before old Schwarz's eyes, like a terrier baiting a great bear.

Yet if anybody knew their stuff when it came to the 'admin', it was Ernie and I for one had no doubt that the papers, at least, would be present and correct.

Willows then offered up some more forms – there was some signing, more brandy, some coffee and much shaking of hands.

'Let us now get our guests accommodated,' said Mumme, in comparatively good English. And this time with a most definite click of the heels, he held out his hand and invited me to precede him down the companion-ladder.

Clarry, I noticed, remained behind and, with his arm about Schwarz's shoulders, was deeply engaged in conversation.

At the quayside were gathered a dozen or so flat-capped, full-bellied men. Most were smoking and those that were not just stood about idly with their hands in their pockets.

'The work force,' said Willows, disparagingly. 'That's why I was late. The drivers and crew could load this lot easily, but the "Union Rules"! Without an extra thirty pairs of hands, we wouldn't be allowed to start. God only knows what use they'll be!'

'Don't look much like stockmen,' I commented.

'Stockmen!' said Willows, with a grunt. 'They've even negotiated danger money. I ask you . . .!'

I shook my head, as if equally disgusted by their action, but somewhere in the back of my mind I remembered Clarry's appraisal of Chester: 'Not one of his best days,' he had said. Perhaps the dockers were not so indolent as they looked, leastways, not when it came to evaluating a job!

'"British Disease",' observed Mumme, sarcastically, having overheard Willows' comments.

I turned to find him standing behind me on the edge of the hatch, about a foot or so higher. He looked quite immaculate, now dressed in a pair of well pressed green overalls, his officer's hat set squarely on his head.

In his right hand he clutched a pair of red rubber gloves, whilst in his left he held what appeared to be a hand torch with no bulb; instead, two metal terminals protruded. It was an electric cattle goad.

'You won't need that,' I said. 'They all lead.'

Mumme looked down upon me from his perch.

'We shall see about that,' he said in a clipped tone. 'Maybe it will help your workers to come to life!'

I had to admit that he might have a point, despite his cynicism.

Mumme then turned his attention to George who was just about to push a rather dilapidated bicycle down the gangway.

'*Wohin gehen Sie?*' he called.

'*An die Apotheke, für den Skip!*' George shouted back.

'Why *der Kapitan* wants to use the chemist, when we haf a Doktor on board, I do not know!' exclaimed Mumme, dropping down beside me. 'And how I am supposed to load a ship with the crew running errands, I also do not know!' He slapped the red gloves impatiently across his thighs. '*Schnell! Schnell!*' he shouted at George, who gave an American-style salute, leaped upon the rickety bicycle and pedalled furiously away up the dock.

Mumme then descended to the bottom of the gangway, which had now been strengthened and the sides boarded. Standing there was a giant of a man, clad in a fisherman's high-necked sweater, waterproof trousers and a pom-pom hat, from beneath which flowed long blond hair. He must have stood six foot six tall and looked to weigh about seventeen stone – quite massive he was, and Scandinavian from his looks.

He was in fact Danish, one Horst Svenson by name, who had had quite a mixed career, even though just in his early twenties. He had recently joined the ship after leaving a fishing trawler in Iceland and had also served some time in the Foreign Legion. His companion, a small dark, greasy little fellow, dressed in similar style to George, but without a beret, was Aristos the Greek. He was reputed to speak six languages and seemed of a slightly nervous disposition, constantly attempting to straighten the thinning strands of heavily oiled hair that lay in a disorganised fashion across his pale scalp.

I was about to make my way down as well, when the bulkhead door behind me slammed, followed by a high-pitched voice:

'Hey, man! Where's de action?'

This was my first encounter with Jimmy the cabin boy, an expatriate Ethiopian.

The only other member was the engineer, who rarely surfaced from the engine room, where he kept the 500 horse-power, Perkins diesel engine in condition.

'We are ready to load, Doktor!' It was Mumme, calling from the quayside.

'I would like to inspect the quarters first,' I answered.

The First Mate frowned rather irritably at my request.

'They are all right, Doktor. You may take my word for it.'

'Would you mind if I took a look myself?' I insisted.

A couple of years amid the Herefordshire farming community, especially with clients like Paxton, had at least given me a degree of confidence when it came to my professional authority. If I was going to be in charge of the welfare of the cattle, I would do it my way, I decided – Third Reich or no!

'So!' muttered Mumme.

He remained, staring at the ground for a few seconds, then looked across towards Horst and Aristos, who had sensed the slight discord and were eagerly anticipating the next parry.

It came from Mumme:

'So!' he repeated, this time emphasising his annoyance at the questioning of his procedure by twice slapping his thigh with the red gloves. 'The Doktor wishes to inspect the hold!' Then, without raising his head, he nodded as if that was just the sort of thing he could expect from a land-based vet. One more slap with the gloves and he pulled himself swiftly back up the gangway.

'This way, Doktor, if you please!' he said, as he passed – rather in the patronising manner of a hotel manager showing a difficult guest to his room.

But below deck, Mumme was right, rather as I had expected – the quarters were well prepared.

The cattle were to be accommodated on two levels in gated pens of various sizes. Gangways between enabled fodder to be distributed and fresh water was supplied from standpipes to portable metal troughs, hung on the pen rails.

Ducted air ventilation, straw bedding over drained concrete floors and fluorescent lighting completed the floating stable; despite my initial impressions of *Dagmar Hansen*'s size, her capacity was deceptive and I could now see how so many cattle could be carried without undue congestion.

Mumme walked ahead, stopping occasionally to give me an enquiring glance.

'Where do you intend to put the bulls?' I asked.

'There are several pens on the lower deck,' he said, leading down the second ramp.

'Couldn't they be housed on the first floor?'

I was thinking about Chester and that he might not be too keen to go right down into the bowels of the ship. Also, the airflow away from the hatch area could well be less and I did not want any respiratory complications if I could avoid them.

'Ve haf already arranged for them to be below!' retorted Mumme firmly; his German accent becoming more accentuated by his attitude.

The bull pens were at the far end of the lower deck, on the starboard side, but as there seemed plenty of room for just two bulls, I did not argue.

'We will keep some empty pens between the boys and the girls,' said Mumme, smiling for the first time. '*Ja?*'

'Good idea,' I agreed.

'Are you happy?' he enquired.

I nodded. 'Thank you.'

'My pleasure, Doktor,' he replied, with an accompanying body salute – and we returned to the deck.

'I think we should load the heifers that are in early pregnancy first,' I suggested. 'Those that are in a more advanced state should then follow on without too much upset. The bulls we'll leave until last . . .'

Mumme nodded, this time in a rather more co-operative manner, and I felt that a rapport had been established, despite the slight initial skirmish.

Of course, as First Mate, Mumme was ultimately responsible under ship's regulations for the safety of the cargo, whether it was cows or cornflakes. Yet, as a veterinary surgeon, I had an equal responsibility and if there was any variance in opinion as to how matters should be handled, it was going to be an interesting question as to who should have the final say.

Horst and Aristos strawed down the ramp as the first lorry backed up. The dockers, still devoid of any visible enthusiasm, moved back, whilst the drivers, themselves all competent stockmen, gathered round purposefully, presenting quite a different approach altogether.

The tailboard was lowered, the folding gates swung back and the first bunch of Herefords were ready to put their last foot – or feet – on their homesoil, before their great adventure.

Because, over the past month, they had been subject to tuberculin and blood testing, various examinations and treatments, they were not unused to being driven and were quite accustomed to a 'follow my leader' approach when it came to alleyways and ramps. So, apart from an initial hesitation and a wary sniff at the sea air, once the bolder ones moved off the others soon followed.

In fact it was quite fun to watch them, for one could sense that they already appreciated a degree of new-found freedom after being cooped up for the previous month, within the confines of the quarantine station at Worlton.

'The lassies are lookin' forrard tae it!' observed Clarry, who had just returned from depositing a package in one of the lorry cabs and, recognising my rather suspicious look, countered my inquisitiveness in a low tone.

'Just encouraging a wee bit o' international trade,' he whispered into my ear. 'Consolidatin' my liquid assets, ye might say!'

Good old Clarry – a true Glaswegian, and no mistake.

The loading progressed extremely smoothly, without any necessity for anything other than vocal persuasion. No sticks were evident and Mumme's electric goad, superfluous.

By twelve o'clock the heifers were safely aboard.

There just remained the two bulls.

Chester and Lucky had been brought down in a separate wagon, driven by Dick Clapstick, a bespectacled old haulier, well known about the county for his cheerful banter.

''Ave the little un' off first,' he called. 'Then the big fella!'

Led by Dick, Wormcastle Lucky Chance walked off the lorry and up the gangway without a qualm, head held high as he looked about, taking in every detail of the new environment. Only at the top of the strawed way did he momentarily halt before going on deck, where he looked back just to ensure that Chester was following.

'Hold up, Dick!' shouted Phil Glossop, one of the Worlton stockmen. 'Till I bring 'im out!'

Then, together with one of the drivers, he went back into the wagon to get Chester.

There was a bit of a scuffle and a few shouts of: 'Come on, matey. Now don't you be silly!' and then with Phil Glossop in attendance with the halter, and the driver holding a fine cord attached to his nose-ring, Chester appeared.

At the edge of the truck, he halted, his eyes roaming the surroundings suspiciously. Slowly he turned his great head from right to left, pulling both his guardians momentarily off balance as he did so.

His presence stimulated, for the first time, some reaction amongst the Newpool dockers, who advanced cautiously to line the gangway, making ribald comments and comparisons about Chester's private parts, as they did so.

The great bull continued to observe the scene, but despite coaxing and cajoling by Phil and the driver, refused to put a foot on the ramp leading down from the lorry.

The efforts gradually assumed a more urgent character, the halter and cord were tugged, language deteriorated and someone passed a cane walking-stick up. I saw Mumme climb onto the back wheel of the wagon and peer through the slats in the body work.

I was on the point of going forward myself, when there came a shout: 'What's the hold-up?' – and at the top of the ship's gangway, having just emerged from an inspection of the pens, appeared MacLowell, Divisional Veterinary Officer of Newpool, complete with black regulation mackintosh, sou'wester and boots, all glistening and stinking of disinfectant!

Whether it was the sight of the 'man in black' or a surreptitious poke in the bum by Mumme and his electric goad, I shall never know – but what happened next will be remembered by the dockers of Newpool for many a long year.

Certainly, the DVO of the Ministry never got a verbal explanation to his enquiry, for from the second the words left his mouth, there was a hold-up no longer.

Chester saw to that!

The great bull took in a gigantic breath that instantly seemed to enlarge his formidable hulk twofold. Then he made three powerful strides down the ramp, dragging Phil and the driver with him like puppets on a string. Halting just long enough to give a snort like the Coronation Scot getting up steam, he took two paces back and, just as he had done at Worlton, drove his massive head into the partition on which the dockers were leaning.

The boarding flew into the air and separated like leaves

on an autumn wind, each one appearing to have a man clinging to it.

Caps flew, fags fell out of mouths, the soles of boots came into view – but Chester had only just started.

Transferring his forward weight from left to right, he gave the same treatment to the other side, completing the operation by lashing out with his hind legs, in a style that would have been the envy of a bucking bronco.

Now both sides of the temporary corral between the lorry and the ship lay in splinters.

The collapse had also pulled over the railed portion of the gangway and Dick Clapstick only just got Lucky aboard in time, leaving Chester standing triumphant on the quay, like a prize fighter who had just smashed his way out of a cardboard box.

With a final flick of his head, he despatched Phil and the driver to the floor behind him.

Chester was free!

He looked around eagerly at the options open to him. If he went left, he could quite easily finish off the majority of the dock workforce; if he went right, he could go home!

Chester went right, and set off at a steady trot for the main gate, with his great tree-trunk of a tail swinging happily behind him.

As I watched him go, a sickening cramp hit my stomach.

The old Devil had done it on me. Now, instead of a substitute, we had no bull at all!

'Sorry! I lost him!'

'*Lost my bull!*' I could see Paxton exploding like an overripe melon.

'Told ye so, laddie!' I could have understood that from Clarry, but he did not criticise. He just stood at my shoulder whistling 'Run Rabbit, Run', in time to Chester's lolloping and fast-disappearing step.

If there were to be any repercussions, it was my fault. It was I who had ultimately accepted him for the trip.

What a Transit Vet! Lost a bloody animal even before we got to sea! And all because I had become too involved.

Why on earth had I decided to bring him in the first place, if I knew he was likely to give trouble? You can not feel sorry for a bull missing a trip abroad – it would not have made one jot of difference to Chester himself, whether he went or not. And how was he to know that his fun and games were cocking up an export deal? He was having a great time!

'Hugh Lasgarn, you're a fool!' I told myself. Fancy deciding to give a bull, who had demolished half a quarantine station, a second chance! I must have been out of my tiny veterinary mind!

Meanwhile Chester had covered quite a bit of ground.

There were several half-hearted attempts by some of the personnel to arrest the absconder's progress – but even in Wales, where the tackling of giants on the rugby field comes as second nature, Chester sailed on, unhindered.

How they could have done with him at Cardiff Arms Park at the Internationals. The thought of his great hulk hurtling through the English pack, scattering the white shirts to all sides as he had done with the dockers, tickled my fancy.

The dockers, however, muttering oaths and threats of reprisal, had started to reassemble, sorting out their caps and fags and rubbing down their bruises.

'That's the fastest they've shifted since they introduced free tea!' said the agent, who himself had just emerged from behind the stack of bales.

''E'll 'ave to stop at the gate, to give 'is name!' chuckled Dick Clapstick. In fact, a general air of jollity seemed to be developing, whether through relief that Chester had gone off in the opposite direction or through genuine amusement, I was not sure.

Then it struck me that, apart from Ernie, who did not personally have to face the consequences of arriving with a bull short on the other side – the problem was entirely mine!

'What got into him?' It was MacLowell, DVO Newpool.

99

At that moment I could have told him quite plainly – but as I might want to work for the Ministry again on my return, I refrained.

Ernie's Austin was nearest.

'Bring your lorry!' I shouted to Dick. 'You can load up some of them, to help.' I motioned toward the bunch of dockers.

Dick looked over the tops of his glasses at me, but made no comment.

'Ve are sailing at 17.00 hours, Doktor!' called Mumme, his face barely suppressing a smile of cynical satisfaction at my plight. 'Othervise he vill haf to swim!'

By the time we reached the end of the warehouse, behind which Chester had disappeared, there was no sign of him. Yet it was obvious he had passed that way from the faces of various bystanders and the positions of safety to which they had suddenly flown – climbing doors, crates and gantries or peeping from behind packing cases.

From the high-rise stern of the *Wakatiki*, half a dozen sailors had a grandstand view and were jumping up and down with excitement, pointing to the open door of the second large warehouse.

As we pulled alongside, I noticed that the sliding panel was not only buckled, but had been wrenched from its runners, and a board which read 'PRIVATE. DEFINITELY NO ADMISSION', had been dislodged.

Chester had passed that way!

But within the great shed there was no sign of him – just an avenue of disaster, leading to another sliding door at the far end, which seemed buckled as well, but in reverse manner.

I think they were bales of raw cotton or some such material that had received the treatment, for the scene gave the impression of a sudden blizzard, through which a hundred frantic reindeer had been hectically driven!

Yet, still there was no sign of Chester!

Around the back of the big sheds, threading our way between trucks and wagons, we finally emerged at the far end of the West Quay.

I got out and gazed despairingly about.

'There he is!' shouted Clarry. 'My God! He's goin' tae dive in!'

Heart in my mouth, I followed his pointing finger to the other side, where a pier, some hundred yards long, ran out into the dock basin – and there, still going at the trot, was Chester. Head up, tail swishing, giving an occasional delighted buck, and heading straight for the water!

Despite my overall concern for the success of the shipment, I had to admit that the wayward rascal looked a picture of pure happiness – like a kid out of school.

And why not? For once in his life, he was really free! No bars, rings, ropes or halters. Just the sea in the distance, sea air in his lungs and not a fence or gate in sight. Even if he knew it would not last for ever, whilst it did, he was determined to enjoy it to the full.

But to my horror, as he neared the end of the pier, he did not even slacken pace and it looked as if he must either fall or jump into the murky water around him. Mumme's words about swimming to Finland might yet be realised!

Then a minor miracle occurred, for perched on top of a marker light at the pier end was a great black-backed seagull, who had watched Chester's jaunty approach from the minute he had stepped onto the no-exit avenue.

Maybe it was the seagull's personal territory; maybe the bird had never seen a bull before – or, just possibly, it was sent for the one particular purpose of saving my skin. All I know is that, with a piercing screech, it flew down at Chester, great wings fully spread – and stopped him dead in his tracks!

However, we still had to get Chester back to the ship and, as we moved closer to the scene, the logistics of the situation became even more frightening.

One tonne of mischievous muscle and blood, riding on a high, standing on a narrow projection surrounded by sea, with not the slightest intention of co-operating with anyone or anybody.

'Got a problem, Mr Lasgarn?' Willows had come up behind.

'Right in one!' I said. 'Any ideas?'

'Landing party to the far end of the jetty, scale the wall and drive him forward,' he suggested. 'But first we'll have to clear it with the Port Authority and as to who'll be prepared to do it – that's another matter.'

It was a sensible suggestion and I, for one, was willing to go; but if Chester decided to play hard to get, all the would-be 'assault force' could quickly end up, back whence they came – in the drink!

No, a 'commando' type raid would take far too long and, personally, I did not think the assembled company were quite in that class.

Backing up a truck towards him, in the hope that he could be coaxed inside, was another dodgy idea that was offered; chances were, however, it would force Chester into the water and, in the mood he was in, he was quite likely to take the occupants with him as well. If the inevitable happened and he did fall in, fishing him out was beyond my comprehension. If, however, we just waited for him to walk back, we could well miss the boat. Checkmate! I was absolutely flummoxed.

Then along came George.

His arrival was heralded by the clattering of the ancient bicycle over the uneven surface; with beret askew, overalls flapping and his clogs at right angles to his line of direction, he looked like a French onion-seller, without his onions. Seeing the gathered crowd, he slowed his rickety steed and looked over to where Chester was facing his would-be captors.

By now, Chester appeared to be in danger of losing his sense of humour. So far his attitude had been one of carefree abandon, but one sensed a degree of meanness was creeping in. His facial expression had deepened, and occasionally he swept the ground backwards with his left forefoot – as he had done at Worlton, when he had covered both Clarry and me in sodden bedding.

102

George stopped. One clogged foot steadied his posture as he gazed with rapt attention at the silhouette of the great bull, standing at the end of the promontory.

For some considerable time, the little seaman stood transfixed; only occasionally did he lower his head and shake it wistfully, giving a low whistle, manifested by his undoubted astonishment.

Slowly he pushed his bike forward, entranced by what he saw.

'Is that some bull!' he said, still eyes fixed upon Chester. 'Never have I seen such a one.'

'Neither have I,' I said, but for very different reasons. 'And I don't want to see another one like him, either. How the hell are we going to get him off there?'

'I get him,' said George. 'You see.'

With that, before I could even consider his actions, he had jumped on his bike and set off down the jetty, towards Chester.

'George!' I shouted. 'Don't be daft!'

'Bloody idiot,' said Clarry.

But there was no stopping him – and he rode on.

Chester watched him all the way.

Probably he could not quite believe his eyes at what he was seeing, and neither could anyone else. The great bull snorted and shook his head, as if a swarm of bees was worrying him.

'He'll kill him,' said the DVO of Newpool. 'Better get an ambulance ready.'

For once, I agreed with the Ministry, as Chester pawed ominously with his forelegs – a right and a left in rapid succession, as if tuning up for a charge.

'I'll back the lorry up. Block this end off,' said Dick. 'If he does go for 'im, 'e'll run on down 'ere an we might just box 'im.'

'Leave it a minute,' I said, without taking my eyes off George as he neared the end of the pier. 'Don't make any noise.'

David and Goliath – it was a unique sight; something

one's mind could hardly conjure up, even in a fantasy. The setting: a stage surrounded by water and now lit by shafts of winter sunshine streaking through the grey clouds. The actors: Goliath, in the form of a massive Hereford bull called Chester, and George, in clogs and beret, who had spent three years in a 'butcher's house'. As we watched in agonised silence from the main quay, the drama unfolded.

George dismounted about ten yards away from the great snorting hulk, took off his beret and, rather like a matador, introduced himself with a sweep of his headgear and a short bow; his stumpy figure not permitting the full elegance of authentic obeisance.

I could hear him talking, but could not quite pick up what he was saying. Whatever it was, it seemed to make little impression on Chester, who continued his war dance, adding to the repertoire his hindquarter bucks.

But his antics steadied at George's next gesture.

Replacing his beret, George picked up the bike by its frame and turned it over, so that it was sitting, upside-down, on the handlebars and saddle.

I was absolutely mystified – and so was Chester, who even took a pace backwards, seemingly unsure of the developments.

Still chatting away, George went to the far side of the up-turned bike and sat cross-legged on the wet stone surface, opposite the crank and pedals.

He continued to chat and, as he talked, he slowly started to turn the crank and put the rear wheel into motion, while with his right hand he revolved the front wheel.

It was unbelievable, even unreal, but if all of us standing on the quay were mesmerised by the spectacle – so was Chester!

The bull took another step backwards and, for a second, I thought he was going to charge, but he did not. Instead, he stretched out his great neck and, still at a good yard, sniffed at the bike with extreme caution.

George continued with his turning, chattering away all the time, but gradually he increased the speed of the revolutions until the whirring of the spokes could be quite clearly heard, even from where we were standing.

Chester became even more fascinated by the spectacle and took a tentative pace forward, his eyes now fixed on the rotating wheels – there was no doubt about it, he was in a trance. Hypnotised by an old bike!

His head moved slowly from side to side as he transferred his gaze from one wheel to the other. Occasionally, he rolled back his upper lip and shut his eyes, as if the experience was sheer ecstasy. I really could not believe my eyes at the transformation; but there was more to come.

George got to his feet and moved round the bike to Chester's side, standing just a foot or so away. He fumbled in his overall pocket for a few seconds, then withdrew something. He put whatever it was to his nose, then sniffed it.

Chester followed his every move, closely.

Then he offered it to the bull.

Once again Chester took a backward step and my heart leaped as he lowered his head. But, following a gentler blowing of hot air through his nostrils, he reached forward and took what lay in George's palm, with one sweep of his curling tongue.

Over the next five minutes, George fed several handfuls of the mysterious substance to Chester, who licked his lips vigorously after each tasting. Whatever it was, it looked as if he was hooked.

Then, completely ignoring his adversary, George turned his back and righted his bike, pointing it in our direction. Without so much as a glance behind, he reached back and, after a few exploratory grasps, took hold of Chester's halter which had been hanging loosely, together with the nose-cord.

I watched dumbfounded as George started to come off the pier, pushing his bike with one hand and leading Chester with the other.

As the little procession came closer, the onlookers parted, not in panic as before, but more in wonderment at the spectacle.

When just a few yards off, I gave a directional sign with

my arm towards the truck where Dick had already lowered the ramp.

But George shook his head and, with Chester in tow, walked right past it and on down the quay to the *Dagmar Hansen*.

And that is how Chester was loaded, making the rest of the departure seem quite ordinary, although for me it was still a novel experience.

We slipped the lock, caught the tide and, by 19.00 hours, were down the Barry Roads in a calm sea, with but one lone seagull following in our wake. Whether it was the one that had uncannily saved the situation back at the dock, I could not tell.

Later that evening I was able to search out George to thank him properly.

'You never learned a trick like that in the "butcher's house", George,' I said.

He rubbed his bristly features with the back of his hand.

'Nay, nay,' he said, grinning. 'I have many jobs; one I work in circus. They call me Gumbo.'

'Gumbo?'

'De clown,' he explained. 'I do dat trick to de big cats.'

I shook my head in amazement.

'What about the mixture you gave him?'

'Skip's medicine, for de stomach,' he said, holding out some grains of brown powder in his hand.

I sniffed it – it was an antacid. But there was a special ingredient that had tickled the great bull's palate: liquorice! One of the main spicing additives of cattle food.

'Skip, he pretty mad I use it for bull,' said George. 'Without it, he like bull himself.'

'That'll make three of them aboard,' I said. 'Instead of one short, we'll have one too many.'

'With you and me, we can soon alter that for him,' said George, with a wicked grin. 'Come haf some coffee.'

And, chuckling at the thought of what the mighty Captain Schwarz would think of the idea, we both went off to the galley.

# 7

A southerly in the Bristol Channel had made for a tiring start to the voyage, my body only slowly acclimatising to the movement as we gradually bobbed out of sight of the Costa del Cardiff.

We severed the last link with the homeland when the pilot, a little fat man called Parry, left the *Dagmar* rather precariously just off the Breaksea Lightship, after availing himself of a quick consultation about his terrier's anal glands before disembarking.

My cabin was situated on the aft skip-deck; it was box-like, adequate and quite claustrophobic. There was a bunk, with faded orange curtains on big brass rings, that gave only a modicum of privacy; a desk; a locker; a basin with hot and cold water and a sea view on two sides.

Every drawer had either a lock without a key, or a key that would not work. But by countless ingenious improvisations, the previous occupant had secured every moving part with either paper wedges, string, wire or elastic. Without these aids, the ship's motion could, in a very short time, give the cabin an appearance of having been 'turned over' in gangster fashion.

On the wall at the foot of the bunk, the previous occupant had left a photograph of a large naked Swedish lady, sitting in a most unusual way on a white chair.

Its presence was quite disturbing within the confines of such a small environment and presented me with one of my first major decisions aboard: should I take it down or not?

To remove the lady for the duration of the voyage was, I felt, a rather prudish action, especially for a Glasgow graduate; alternatively, one had to admit, it was a pleasant but constant distraction.

Finally, it was old 'Bomber' Bardsley, Professor of Pathology in my University days, who came to the rescue; how unknowingly useful his lectures were, especially when I remembered his pronouncement:

'It is impossible to build up a tangible resistance without a major involvement with the antagonist.'

Of course, he was talking about the development of bodily immunity, and, if one stretched the point slightly, there was, in my case, a need to develop an immunity from the body in question. So, when I came back after my final inspection of the cattle, I lay upon my bunk and studied the poster for some time, on the principle that it was the most logical way of developing a resistance to its effect.

Whether it was the influence of the lady or the capriciousness of the Atlantic rollers as we neared Land's End I am unsure, but after a fitful night's sleep, I discovered on waking that I was half an hour late for breakfast, ship's time being one hour ahead of local.

Leaping from my bunk, the antics of the floor caused me to grab the hand-rail to steady myself, and dressing in the prevailing conditions was quite a hilarious performance. When my clothes and I finally joined company I lunged out of the cabin and down to the mess room.

It was empty, the meal having already being taken – a situation which caused me to breakfast alone and, for the first time, to become aware of Gustav Brandt's problem.

Although, over the coming years as a sea-going vet, I was to meet a variety of ship's cooks, Gustav was definitely of the lower echelon. His appearance would have made any selfrespecting members of his profession weep into their Coq-au-Vin. He wore what could best be described as a faded pair of crumpled pyjamas. The jacket of the ensemble had a suggestion of a thin blue stripe running through it, whilst the buttons grimaced in an attempt to avoid his fat stomach advancing to upset his total equilibrium. Below, baggy pants shrouded black clogs on which he noisily shuffled about his culinary business. Hair reminiscent of a wind-torn, straw-roofed barn topped a pale face that merged with the tired uniform, interrupted only by a scraggy ginger-tinged beard, through a hole in which he continuously mumbled.

That morning, whilst deliberating as to my next move, Gustav appeared in all his dishevelled glory at the mess-room door, arms folded across the ledge of his abdomen. His right arm was adorned by a dismasted version of the *Cutty Sark*; while, on his left, from biceps to wrist, a giant blue fish with a pair of female legs protruding from its jaws parodied the old Biblical tale.

Waving away my apologies with the *Cutty Sark*, he motioned me to the small wall-fixed table. Then he disappeared.

Suddenly he was there again, banging a plate of lightly fried eggs before me.

I contemplated the sight as it rose and fell with the ship's motion; if there was a Loch Ness monster, it would surely have eyes like these, I thought. But before I could come to any firm decision regarding the jaundiced optics, Gustav thudded heavily into the opposite seat, his shaky hand clutching a mug from which protruded the bent handle of a spoon. Then he fixed me with his tiny sunken eyes and said slowly, in broken English:

'I haf a poker.'

Conversation on foreign cattle boats is not always easy, but I adopted the ploy of repeating the statement, giving myself more time to attempt an interpretation.

'You have a poker,' I confirmed, smiling.

My playing for time, however, shed little light on Gustav's statement.

'*Ich habe ein Poker*,' I tried, wondering what the translation from German could be. If it was similar to English, the conversation could get out of hand in several ways.

There followed an uneasy silence, and then I was conscious of the engines throbbing, the ship rolling and the eggs grinning from the plate beneath.

As I reached for my cup, my hand froze in mid-air, for Gustav suddenly flattened his nose, compressed his shoulders and emitted a violent snort.

Then, all became clear.

'Porker! Pig!' I exclaimed thankfully.

'*Schwein!*' Gustav stood up triumphantly, '*Ein Schwein!*'

He stood up unsteadily, mug in hand.

'*Kommen Sie!*' he commanded.

Thankful for any excuse to escape the leering, yellow-eyed monsters before me, I followed him through to the galley.

Despite his personal appearance, Gustav's galley was orderly and clean. There were two large cooking stoves for'ard and a sink and draining board on the starboard wall. Pots and pans hung in gay abandon and a giant kettle, clamped to a burner, gasped intermittently as it lurched to and fro.

Turning away, Gustav faced a table to aft and, bending, opened the cupboard doors beneath.

'Here iss *mein Schwein*,' he announced, 'an diss iss *das Schweinhaus!*'

I must still have been somewhat disorientated, because before I could register amazement, I found myself bending down and looking into the cupboard. I had not really expected to see a *Schwein*; in fact, all I saw were rows of tins, large and small, bearing German descriptions of their contents: *Mohrrübe im Salzwasser* and *Blumenkohl mit Kräuter* – alarming to the ignorant, but containing nothing more sinister than carrots in brine and cauliflower with herbs.

Gustav closed the cupboard, stood up and said quietly: 'Das iss Greta, mein darling.' Then he walked out of the galley and into his cabin, which was directly opposite, and slammed the door.

I stood alone amongst the swinging saucepans, watching the fat kettle grunting on the hob and the dishmop nodding its unkempt head in a pot by the sink.

The Ancient Mariner's 'silly buckets on the deck' became a reality, and I felt a trifle uneasy.

Recovering, I remembered I had other responsibilities aboard and decided to see if I could get more sense out of the Herefords, little realising that I had not 'seen' the last of Greta the Phantom Pig.

During the next five days, *Dagmar*, the floating cowshed, ploughed steadily on around Land's End, where the Atlantic breakers played shuttlecock with her tiny frame, giving us all, crew and cattle alike, a bit of a shake-up.

My assumptions regarding the three 'C's were surprisingly accurate, for there was little water intake amongst the cattle during the early stages, which compounded the constipation but was soon remedied by feeding bran. Epsom Salts was used in some of the more 'concrete' cases to great advantage.

Because of the rough passage off Cornwall, the hatches were battened and the atmosphere in the hold developed rather more humidity than expected, despite the ventilation system sucking the stale air up through the giant 'drain-pipes'.

It was worrying on two counts: firstly an outbreak of coughing developed, but this was also accompanied by running eyes and noses, which made the cattle look decidedly unhealthy.

I watched carefully for signs of secondary pneumonia and took temperatures of any suspects regularly. Seven cattle gave cause for concern, three of them being among the more heavily pregnant heifers and, because of this, I decided to embark upon preventative treatment.

Of those with eye trouble, a dressing of ophthalmic ointment twice daily was given to prevent any permanent damage to the corneal surface. George was my clinical assistant and ever willing to undertake any task to which he was delegated. Dressing the eyes was done on the main clinical inspection of the day, starting after breakfast. Each animal was carefully scrutinised and any abnormality recorded in my log; treatments were carried out as we worked through.

As for restraint, the heifers could be held by the horns to

111

steady them up, but Lucky, who had developed quite a bad conjunctivitis and who, like Chester, was given a pen to himself, needed to be haltered. Try as he would, George could not get this right.

A rope halter is, after all, a loop, a shank and a sliding knot. The poll piece is firstly placed over the horns, with the noose that forms the base of the loop around the muzzle, and the sliding knot on the leading side under the jaw. With the right hand, adjust the shank, which should now be running from the left side of the face, and the bull is haltered. If you see what I mean.

However, there is a knack to it, and either you have it or you have not and George, despite his 'three years in a butcher's house', had not. Each time he tried, and Lucky was extremely patient, he would finish up with the nose band upside-down, the shank pulling from the cheek and not up from the chin, or the whole thing back to front.

'Take the shank and throw it over your left shoulder – hold the sliding knot in your right hand. With your left hand, open the poll piece from the cheek piece and slide it over the horns . . . so!'

I demonstrated the method over and over again.

'I god it!' George would exclaim, grabbing the rope enthusiastically. Then, for reasons known only to himself, he would cross hands, fiddle, pull and finish up with it completely the wrong way round.

'George!' I would say in despair. 'Look! Shank to the left, poll piece over the right horn.'

'Please?' George would enquire with a disarming smile on his rugged features, then hold up his left hand and say: 'To right!'

'NO!'

'Left?'

'YES! LEFT FOR PORT!'

'Ja! Und right für Steerboard?'

'Yes, George! Left for port and right for starboard.'

'So! I take the shanks to Ports and die polling pieces to Steerboard. So! An' pulling shank . . . so! How iss dat?'

'Bravo! You've got it!'

The following day, when the heifers were finished, we made for Lucky's pen. George collected the halter and, with a broad grin on his face, announced confidently:

'Today I ged it!'

With someone who could not tell left from right, I had my doubts, until I saw that George was not relying entirely on my instructions or his improved expertise. For when we came upon Lucky, I discovered that my clinical assistant had left nothing to chance: when Lucky looked up, he had been painted. The tips of his horns were sporting different colours, red and green – the left one red for port and the right, green for starboard. And, for the very first time, George got it right.


When I had finished my work with the stock, I would go up on the bridge.

It was a very efficient area of the ship and needed to be: after all, whether a ship is fifty tonnes or five thousand, the principles of seamanship are basically the same, and the responsibilities of the Captain and First Mate are morally no less on a little ship like *Dagmar* than an ocean liner.

The watches were taken, turn about, by the Captain who took morning and evening, and the Mate who took afternoon and night, each one of six hours duration.

My first visit to the bridge was in the evening.

Schwarz was peering out to the horizon through a pair of gigantic binoculars, one of the major preoccupations of every watch; while at the wheel stood Aristos, steering to the charted course.

'Ah! Doktor!' said Schwarz, completing his scanning. 'Good! Be seated, please!'

He pointed to a high stool at the right of the wheel. It was a precarious position in view of the rolling motion, but, not wanting to appear unco-operative at my first appearance, I obliged.

Aristos, on my left, stood like a statue, his features devoid of all expression.

113

What happened next was, initially, quite disturbing, especially in view of my previous encounter with Gustav and his 'poker'.

The Captain advanced towards me.

'You are putting your hands . . . so!' he ordered.

Schwarz took my hands, placing the left upon the chart desk and the right at the side of a brass barometer, fixed to the wall.

'Now you will be looking . . . so!'

He cupped my chin in his broad hand, screwing it upwards to the left so that my eyes rested directly upon a coffee jug, wedged in a hoop in the corner of the third bridge window.

Schwarz then stood back, clasped his hands and viewed me in the manner of a satisfied Womens' Institute flower arranger, regarding her creation for Harvest Festival.

Once again, I was beginning to feel uneasy about things and would have liked to glance at Aristos, if only for re-assurance. But Schwarz was still observing my position with much thought.

Twice he came forward, each time to adjust the angle of my head.

Finally, he clapped his hands loudly, smiled and said:

'Now, Doktor! You vill be listening!'

With that, he nodded toward Aristos, whom I dared not turn to, and raised both hands above his head, like a High Priest.

He held them in the air for a few seconds, then raising them even higher, he brought them down in a wide outward sweep – and a tumultuous blast of uninhibited Wagner enveloped the whole bridge.

I gasped at the volume of sound which was pouring from the two stereo speakers which I could just glimpse from the corner of my eye – and it was then that the ritual of my positioning became clear. I relaxed my neck muscles, but a glance from Schwarz made me swiftly resume my position and maintain it until the Valkyrie had ridden well past!

114

Apart from the musical interludes on the bridge, which were giving me a most intimate knowledge of the 'Ring Cycle' – something I could well have managed without – I spent some time in my cabin. Not, I might add, leering at my naked Swedish lady, although I did acknowledge her presence whenever I entered, but reading up some of the veterinary medical information relating to the cattle, which I thought might be needed when we reached Finland.

The cabin was kept tidy by a dose of 'Black Man's Magic'. This expression came to me from Jimmy the Ethiopian himself, and it is something that, even to this day, I do not take lightly.

I first heard him use it when I was obliged to amputate the horns of a flighty little heifer that had managed to jump out of her pen, despite the height of the rails. Although she came to no harm from that feat, she had run on to the end of the alleyway and, in an attempt to force her way out, had squeezed between two girders, about eighteen inches apart, and got irretrievably stuck. As she pushed her body forward through the narrow gap, her ribs compressed, but sprang once they were clear of the girder. This meant she could not go further on, because her hips were too wide, or be pushed back, because her chest was too broad.

She was well and truly stuck.

After much discussion about the mechanics of the situation, we were still nowhere near a solution, and I feared that George's expertise, gained from his 'three years in a butcher's house', might well be needed.

Then Horst came upon the scene.

If the proverbial village blacksmith was a 'mighty man', he would have had to go some to match the giant Dane – though, in common with the rural craftsman, he was very gentle with it.

It was Horst who noticed that as the girders ascended to the ceiling of the lower hold, they did get fractionally wider. If it were possible to raise the heifer to that position,

115

she might well have a chance – but how to elevate her? Pulley blocks were of little use, for the roof was solid and there were no attachments. Trying to widen the gap lower down was not possible, for that could well weaken the general structure, which would be dangerous.

Then Horst came out with his solution. 'I will lift her!' he said.

I would never have believed it had I not been there, but the 'mighty man' tightened his wide leather belt, took a gigantic breath, then crouched beneath the heifer's forelegs with his back under her brisket.

With another mammoth inhalation, he tensed his muscles so that they rippled through his T-shirt and, with a roar like frenzied lion, stood up!

The heifer appeared to become suddenly weightless and rose between the girders like a helium-filled balloon, until she was within the wider part of the gap.

As Horst became upright, she started to keel over backwards, her ribcage just able to reverse, allowing her to tumble, exhausted but free, onto her backside.

We all cheered and Horst, in the true manner of a champion weight-lifter, clasped his great hands above his head in triumphant acknowledgement of the feat.

It was a magnificent act and, once again, saved the reputation of the consignment and, not least, that of Hugh Lasgarn, transit vet.

Unfortunately the heifer had cracked a horn, right at its base, lifting it off the skull by a good centimetre, and I knew full well that in the heavy atmosphere of the hold it was unlikely to heal.

Amputation was the logical course.

Great interest was shown by all the crew when I removed the horn under local anaesthetic – even Captain Schwarz left his Wagner and put in a brief appearance. George, attired in what looked uncannily like a butcher's apron, assisted, while Horst used his strength, to restrain the patient.

Jimmy had watched the operation in silence and, when

it was completed, respectfully asked if he could keep the detached portion as a souvenir.

The request was greeted with jibes of witchcraft and other more impolite suggestions by his companions, but he fended off their raucous humour with a fluorescent grin.

'Ah'm needin' three more for de set!' he addressed the jokers, waving the horny appendage before their eyes. 'So youse wise guys best be lockin' yo doors tonight!' He gave a little jig. 'Beware de "Black Man's Magic"!'

For me, however, on that trip, 'Black Man's Magic' was Jimmy's ability to manicure my untidy cabin, whilst I worked below. To fold my clothes, tidy my desk, organise my toiletries about the washbasin and make my bunk into an orderly resting place, instead of the twisted, creased, lumpy pallet from which I emerged each morning.

He called me for meals, told me if any interesting shipping was in view and generally attended to my various requirements with the dedication of an old retainer.

It was Jimmy, too, who heralded the next unforgettable incident of my maiden voyage.

It was three stormy nights later, as I lay in my bunk, attempting to assimilate some of the researches of Messrs Alston and Broom, in their publication *Leptospirosis in Man and Animals*, a disease about which the Finns were particularly concerned, when hurried footsteps up the gangway, followed by three sharp knocks on the cabin door, broke into my meditations.

'*Kommen Sie!*' I shouted.

The door burst open and a body thrust itself into the dimly lit cabin. Jimmy, whose coal-black skin made him difficult to see in the darker areas of the ship at the best of times, entered, his eyes shining as if powered by two super torch batteries.

'Skip say . . . Quickly come! Please, Doktor! It's Gustav!' His thin chest was heaving with relief as he imparted the message.

Used as I was to responding to the midnight calls of

distressed clients without panic, such was the urgency of Jimmy's request that I scorned dressing, and followed him down the gangway, clad only in my pyjamas.

The Captain and Aristos the Greek were peering into Gustav's cabin, whence came stifled yells.

Captain Schwarz stood back when I arrived and, placing a hand on my shoulder, said:

'Gustav iss hafing a liddle turn. He iss saying dat Greta iss sick and he iss wishing that you cure her.'

My facial expression must have prompted the next remark.

'He gets a liddle upset at these times,' he continued. 'But if you humour him, he iss soon okay. Last time iss on der way to Klaipeda for der horses and Gustav say Greta escape – den we must all be pretend look for her. You see, Doktor . . .' he shook his head gravely, 'as a human being, Gustav iss impossible . . . but as a cook, he iss not so bad. So, please, Doktor! Please!'

Edging cautiously around the door, I spied Horst and Karl the engineer, a combined 200 kilos, sitting on a struggling heap that was Gustav.

As I entered the cabin, they eased their weight and Gustav sat up, stroking his tangled hair in a futile attempt to improve his appearance. Then, like a cornered owl, he fixed me with his beady eyes.

For a full minute, he stared, breathing noisily in a crescendo that exploded in a stream of garbled German.

Captain Schwarz stepped forward and silenced him with a firm command. Then, in a modified tone, he explained.

'Gustav say you will be needing your medicine bag. Please, Doktor, to humour him.'

I returned to my cabin, collected my black case containing the requirements for the Herefords, and descended again to the lower deck.

By now Gustav was standing at the door of the galley and greeted me with another stream of unintelligible German.

The Captain translated:

'He iss saying Greta's time iss due for de liddle pigs . . . but der comes nothing!'

Gustav nodded his head in approval and pointed to the empty galley floor.

I looked hard at the Captain, who smiled back and said: 'Please, Doktor.'

'Ja. Please,' pleaded Gustav.

So, into the open space I stepped . . . carefully avoiding treading on my phantom patient that occupied it.

Kneeling, I opened up my case and took out a thermometer. Patting the air where I suspected the hot, bristly flank was most likely to be, I gently inserted the thin glass body into the imaginary rectum.

After a reasonable interval, I retrieved it, studied it carefully and nodded my head in approval of the reading.

'Tell him everything is normal,' I said to the Captain.

Captain Schwarz took a considerable time conversing with Gustav, who kept shaking his head in obvious disbelief.

'He iss thinking der liddle pigs are bigsize and may be stuck,' Schwarz's left eyelid twitched and a faint grin crossed his face. 'He iss asking dat you examine her internally.

I wish I could have seen my face – it must have been a picture!

Gritting my teeth, I knelt down again, only to be roughly yanked to my feet by Gustav.

'He will bring you der hot water and soap first,' came the explanation.

Beginning to feel a bit of a fool at this juncture, I sighed heavily, but the Captain sensed my feelings and placed a hand on my shoulder.

'Please to humour him and he will soon be okay,' he assured.

So, humour him I did and, rolling up my pyjama sleeve, I carefully soaped my arm and gently introduced it into the invisible porcine vagina.

There is no doubt that the instinct a veterinary surgeon

119

acquires from the constant handling of animals never departs. Consequently, I carried out the manoeuvre with all the care I would have accorded the real thing. So much so, that at one point I almost imagined my fingers touching the snout of a largish piglet, just beyond the pelvic brim.

I closed my eyes and, taking care not to push against the rhythmical contractions of the uterine wall, I gradually worked my hands around the slippery head. I had nearly secured it when a distinct pluck backwards took it out of my grasp; but the next contraction passed it deeply into the palm of my hand and gradual traction brought a wriggling, phantom piglet into the big wide world.

I turned to Gustav, who had been kneeling by my side and placed my cupped hands in his.

Looking up at the Captain, I said quietly:

'Tell him I have removed the first piglet. It was large and obstructing the rest. She will be all right now.'

As I rose to dry my hands, Gustav mumbled something.

'He is very grateful. He iss saying he will stay mit her for der night.'

Gustav was still kneeling, back towards me, staring at his cupped hands. There was something very sad and touching in the whole situation, that escaped me in its reasoning.

Picking up my case, I nodded to Captain Schwarz and bade the rest of the company 'Gute Nacht'. Fantasy it may have been, but though I say it myself, it was a good job!

Thankfully reaching the sanity of my cabin, I hauled myself into my bunk, only to feel Alston and Broom sticking into my right side.

Pulling the book out, I idly opened the cover:

'There is no great genius without a tincture of madness,' said a pencilled quotation on the fly leaf.

I pondered the philosophy in the light of the night's events.

'Enough!' I told myself. 'Morning will soon come.'

I glanced blearily at my watch. It read 2.30 am – 02.30 hours, to be correct – another day.

In fact, another month. During the night March had turned to April.

Today was April the First!

I sat bolt upright in my bunk.

Suddenly, my neck was cold. I stared hard at the face of the nude Swedish lady, sitting so adventurously on her white chair.

'They wouldn't do that to me would they?' I asked her.

But she did not answer. She just sat there, smiling sweetly from her perch.

# 8

If I had any misgivings about the authenticity of Gustav's 'problem' and the fact that I might have been the victim of a prank, they could well have been added to when, even before daybreak, there was another frantic hammering upon the cabin door.

This time it was George.

'Quickly! Come quick! Der is borning a liddle one in de caddle!'

After the previous bizarre episode, coupled with my soporific state and the swirling of my brain as I sat up, I was more than a little confused.

'For Pete's sake, George!' I said, irritably. 'Pull the other one!'

'Der udder one?' He blinked. 'No udder one, just de one. Two feets and a nose.'

'But they're not due yet, George?

'Doktor,' said George, 'when de apple is ripe, it is dropping – but if the wind blows, it is dropping early.' He nodded as if to confirm the profundity of his observation.

'Right!' I said, not over-impressed with philosophies of that nature at five in the morning. 'I'll come and see.'

But this time, I dressed first.

'Diss one!' said George, pointing to a petite wide-eyed heifer standing amongst a bunch of five.

I took a look at her rear end, but there seemed little alteration to her anatomy.

'You sure?' I questioned, for if it was another spoof, I was going to get very annoyed.

'Sure,' confirmed George. 'Two feets and a nose.'

'Where, George? Where?'

'Dey were peeping,' said George. 'I see them.'

I looked at the records. The heifer, according to her certification, was not due for another six weeks, but as she had been 'running with the bull', the actual date would be very difficult to determine. This, coupled with the transit, could be responsible for an unauthorised arrival, and as the heifer was also one of those that I had given a preventative injection against pneumonia, I decided I had better investigate.

Before attempting any examination, we moved her into an empty pen and George put on a halter, getting it right first time.

The heifer was very disturbed and danced about, making my approach difficult, but by gentle persistence I was able eventually to slide my soaped arm cautiously into her vagina and onto the head and two 'feets' of the calf.

George was right: there was 'borning a liddle one'!

Being premature, the heifer had not relaxed as she might have if the pregnancy had gone full term, so it was necessary to apply some extra traction. I had not come prepared for calving cases, but fortunately the ship had no shortage of cords and ropes and some aids to the delivery were soon provided; within a few minutes 'Georgina' – for what else could she have been christened? – was born.

The baby calf created an unbelievable interest aboard and it seemed strange that such a delicate mite could touch the tender spots in a tough sea-going crew. There was hardly a moment when one or other was not sneaking down to the hold to take a look at the new arrival.

The mother had very little milk and so a supplementation was necessary; ship's milk was of the 'long life' variety and low in fat and vitamins, so I had to mix a little corn oil and add some vitamin capsules, provided by Mumme, to try and bring it to the right constitution.

The engineer fashioned a rudimentary teat from some soft rubber pipe and, with a Carlsberg Lager bottle holding the milk, the feeding was successful.

To begin with I recommended four-hourly feeds and George took over the responsibilities, though Gustav gave overwhelming assistance, too, mixing and warming the milk and acting as a relief nursemaid.

*　　*　　*

By Sunday night, we were at the mouth of the Elbe and catching the stream, which helped us by two hours; we slotted the little *Dagmar Hansen* amongst a variety of sea-going craft in the Kiel Canal.

The Kiel Canal is the short-cut between the North Sea and the Baltic, a marine motorway that extends 61 kilometres from Brunsbüttel in the south to Kiel in the north, and it was a blessed respite during the voyage, although the cattle became noticeably unsettled by the smell of land.

It was dawn as we chugged gently through the still waters; the clouds were thin, heralding a bright spring morning, and, as we passed, I watched the dainty chalets opening their sleepy shutters, the world waking up on bicycles and toy trains crossing the great iron bridges.

We bunkered at Kiel and I posted a card home, with the enthusiasm of an exile of many years – though so far, for the cattle and me it had been just six days! We took on oil, water and Carlsberg Lager, food, equipment, mail and more Carlsberg Lager.

At mid-day on the Monday, the great gate of the North Lock slid mightily open, discharging us into the Baltic Sea, but alas, only at eight knots, and soon our canal companions were just twinkling silhouettes in the distance.

So far the voyage had been rough, but certainly not unbearable, and I was enjoying every minute of the experience, looking forward to the arrival in Finland and to making new acquaintances.

The gale warning came at 13.00 hours on the Tuesday.

It was written on a pad headed *Nachrichten für Seefahrer*.

The signal read:

NORTH WESTERLY. STORM FORCE TEN.
IMMINENT

Even I knew that when gales at sea turned to storms it was no place to be! I comforted myself by thinking it might not be quite as bad as it sounded, that it might be local and miss our course completely, but it had said 'IMMINENT' and things were certainly starting to happen.

Cattle boats ride high in the water, unlike tankers or heavier vessels, and, instead of ploughing through the waves, float like corks on the surface... But corks can also bob and *Dagmar* was beginning to do just that.

In those short grey hours of Baltic daylight, the scene changed from light entertainment to a horror movie, with full sound accompaniment.

The sea became a turmoil: first the waves towered above us, then we towered above the waves, as if on a giant roller-coaster. Darkness fell like a blanket and the ship continued to screw and squirm, and I could not stand or sit or lie in that crazy spin-drier.

The distorted equilibrium of simple things, like books and spoons and cups and boots, made no sense, and God only knows how long I hung onto that cabin rail.

Only the naked Swedish lady seemed unperturbed.

It was the sight of a book that appeared to be in the first stages of weightlessness, that reminded me of something I had read: 'Positive thought leads to positive action in adversity.' Now was the time to try it!

Positive thought: Who was I and what was I doing here?

Reply: I was a veterinary surgeon in charge of a cattle transit.

Positive action: I would go and see the cattle.

I attempted to make my way down to the hold, which had to be done by ladders leading through the engine room.

After a series of drunken acrobatics, I eventually arrived and flopped on a stack of bales in front of the bull pens.

Chester had adopted a sitting-dog position, having wedged himself at an angle in the pen; this gave him maximum support and a low centre of gravity. His eyes were half-closed, presenting the appearance of a large, white-faced, hairy Buddha with horns.

Lucky was recumbent, his head under the straw. The heifers, some standing, some lying, had a helpless look on their faces that enhanced their femininity.

I pulled my way along the rails to where Georgina was lying, partitioned off from her mother by a small gate; the little calf was fast asleep and oblivious to it all!

The noise pattern in the hold was weird. The waves were throwing the ship forward, so that the propeller left the water on every second wave. As the blades flailed the waterless void, the hull juddered in tetanic spasm; then, for about four seconds, absolute silence as if we were sailing through space – followed by crash, thunder, roll, pitch and the whole devilish cycle started again.

My positive thought began to weaken... 'Would it ever end and, if it did, when and how?... Could the hull stand the strain?... Collisions?... There was a lot of shipping in the Baltic!'

Suddenly, I felt a lump in my throat and, as I stumbled back to the bales by the bull pens, my knees were weak and the cold, clammy hand of fear gripped my heart.

Fear, for me a new sensation. Fright I knew well: such as the time Mika paid her unwelcome attentions to me as I sat in the solitary confinement of the Jolokowski loo; the time I was savaged by Umtali, a neurotic and, unlike Greta, very real sow; or the time I was cornered in a stable, behind the hind legs of a kicking horse.

But fright is transient, fear is not.

To learn about fear I had had to come many miles from the gentle beauty of the Herefordshire countryside to the Baltic Sea, when the barometric pressure plummeted, Force Ten winds screamed hysterically and icy green mountains of foaming sea lashed the little cattle boat *Dagmar Hansen*, fighting to reach the coast of Finland.

For fifteen detached hours that bore no relation to time or date in my shattered senses, nature played a cruel game with the lives of eight crewmen, seventy-nine Hereford heifers, two bulls, a calf called 'Georgina' and one country vet.

It was then that I knew fear.

I was sitting on the bales in a cold sweat, when Chester opened his eyes and raised his head, as if he would have liked to say something ... if he could.

But the look said it all:

'Why the hell did you get me into a situation like this?'

'I thought I was doing you a favour,' I replied, as if he had really spoken.

Chester seemed to shake his head in dismay, then he closed his eyes again, and did not seem bothered at all.

Chester of all creatures, big enough to blast his way out of a concrete bunker; the escapologist of Newpool Docks. Chester, the most unpredictable of all the passengers, the one who could go berserk at the sight of a wet black mackintosh, was as calm and as cool as a cucumber; and I, a level-headed, intelligent, positive-thinking human, was in a state of near hysteria! Why?

Perhaps I had more to lose.

There was the quality of my life against his – or my future; but then, Chester's life had been pretty good so far, feeding and fertilising amid the rolling pastures of Herefordshire.

And as for his future: well, that was certainly more assured than mine, for I knew Paxton had taken the precaution of preserving his blood line, and there was a deep freeze full of the vital ingredient back home, to ensure it.

But even so, why should we worry? There were plenty more vets and plenty more bulls; nobody was indispensable.

And of course, that was it: my fear was based on a selfish, conceited conception of my own importance!

How would they manage, Diana and Sara ... without

me? *Could* they manage? Of course they could. The trouble was – I was afraid of *not* being missed.

Animals like Chester, despite their tantrums, did not know fear like humans because they were not selfish or conceited or full of their own importance . . . but that argument would not hold water . . . *would not hold water*!

I started to laugh, Chester smiled and the heifers giggled and I knew I was going round the bend!

When I awoke, my back was aching, my left leg had cramp and I was wet through; the bales beneath me were also wet, but – the best 'but' of all – the wind had dropped, the ship was steadier and we were making progress.

I broke open some dry bales and ran hay along the front of the pens; only Chester showed any interest. I checked on Georgina who had just awoken and was up and stretching, as if after a good night's sleep. Then I clambered up the iron ladders to the skip-deck.

The contents of my cabin had succumbed to the elements, despite the wedges and string, and lay in complete disarray, as if scattered by a giant fan.

I leaned against the bunk and took out my little notebook, in which I had recorded the events of the voyage so far. My mind still awash, which perhaps accounts for the odd entry for 7th April:

> O miracle of motion, O face that's never still,
> Whose curves and spines oft come and go,
> Whose fragile foam, like scattered snow,
> Can turn and bite with vicious force,
> A peril to man's feeble course.
> Be gentle in your care of me,
> As I am sailing through you . . . Sea.
>
> This little box that I call home,
> That shakes and rattles through the moan
> Of engines far below.
> That now is up and now is down

And then is aft and then is fore,
My mind and body trying to cope
With living on this mad see-saw.

I swear I'll never come again,
Subject myself to all this pain.
O Father, Son and Holy Ghost,
Next time . . . I'll send this lot by post!

The rest of the trip was spent bedding and grooming, and we took our pilot off Hanko the following morning. The little ship threaded her way through the maze of small islands that make up the Finnish Archipelago, a fairyland in spring and summer, but a graveyard for the unwary at any other time.

At the dock, the Finnish veterinary authorities were waiting to inspect the cattle and the documentation – Georgina presenting an immigration problem as she had no papers! The buyers were there, too, including the one with the steely eyes. He led his delegation amongst the pens, with a critical appraisal of the Herefords' condition.

'You have very rough weather, Mr Lasgarn,' he said as we neared the bull pens. I nodded in reply.

Then he turned and looked at Chester.

'The bull, he was very frightened in the storm, no?' he enquired.

And Chester raised his head as if he would have liked to say something . . . if he could!

The cattle disembarked admirably, Chester leading the parade with great style.

Everyone admired him, and I knew then that my decision back at Worlton had been right. Georgina was also a star and the Press photographers were snapping her from all angles.

When the off-loading was completed, I packed my bags ready to follow them to the Quarantine Station at Fagavek, where they would be kept for the next month.

Before I left, I said my goodbyes to everyone: Captain Schwarz, Mr Mumme, Horst, Aristos, Gustav, Hans, the engineer and George.

'It was a happy time, no?' said George, slapping me across the shoulder – and I had to agree.

'Where's Jimmy?' I asked.

'I here, man!' came the reply, and across the deck he walked. Taking my hand he squeezed my palm with his and then pushed into it a small box.

'You take this,' he said, smiling, 'an' remember Jimmy. Cos' Jimmy always remember you!'

I was a little taken aback by the gesture, but the Finns were waiting impatiently on the quay, car doors open, engines revving. I had no time to say anything more than 'Thanks' and 'Goodbye'.

They all waved as I left the little ship *Dagmar Hansen*, the 'floating cowshed' that had braved the storms and the crew that had cared for its passengers, human and bovine, as they do on a 'ladies' liner'.

It was a hard night in Helsinki, with much talking, eating and very much drinking.

I took a sauna, and nearly ruined myself externally; and joined in the toasts of schnapps, and definitely ruined myself internally! But Jack was home from the sea, even if I was in foreign parts; the buyers, even he of the steel-grey eyes, were pleased, and I felt that celebrations were in order.

It was the small hours before I finally found the sanctuary of my hotel bedroom.

Seated on the bed, leg-weary, eyes drooping, I emptied my pockets.

Money, handkerchief, tickets, comb, matchbox ... matchbox? What was I doing with a matchbox? I did not smoke.

It was Jimmy's box.

Holding it in the palm of my right hand, I gently eased away the lid. Inside, nestling on a piece of veterinary cotton-wool, was a tiny, exquisitely carved seagull in flight, fashioned from a heifer's horn – the one he had kept as a souvenir.

A seagull in flight – how uncanny!

I would remember Jimmy, and, as I flew out over the Land of a Thousand Lakes the following day, with a million memories of my first cattle transit, his was well up in front.

# 9

I had originally come to Ledingford for only thirty days, and it was the premature demise of G. R. Hacker MRCVS, the senior partner of the firm, that had unexpectedly prolonged my stay. During the following months I had met and married Diana and now, with our new daughter Sara, was well settled in the County.

The 'export' job coming my way had set the seal on my contentment, for if there was one thing that I mildly regretted – although at the time I had been desperate to avoid it and the risk of being parted from my 'girl on the piano stool' – it was the lifestyle of some of my colleagues who, after qualifying, had joined the Royal Army Veterinary Corps.

There was Scotty Bennet, now in Hong Kong, who sent me occasional bulletins of his progress, that would make a saint envious – if one could believe everything that he wrote. Jamie McLaren had been posted to Fiji, for some obscure reason, and wrote with similarly intriguing news, whilst others were scattered far and wide on Her Majesty's Service, in outposts that made country vetting seem parochial to say the least.

The cattle trips, however, made up for it and satisfied the sense of adventure that I felt I had missed through not joining up.

Coming home from my first expedition, I was probably more excited than before I had gone and was so full of travellers' tales that I could quite understand how sailors got the name for spinning yarns and how seas could get rougher and storms wilder at every telling – although I felt my experience needed no exaggeration.

Diana listened enthusiastically to all I had to say, was

thrilled with the presents and genuinely relieved to have me back safe and sound.

'Mac called by to see if I was all right, and said you were having rough weather,' she said. 'And I did worry. Did you ever feel frightened?'

'It was a bit scary at times,' I admitted, thinking to myself that sailors' yarns can be exaggerated both ways; though deep inside I knew that what I had experienced had been more than just simple fright.

It was great to be home and to relax in a room that was steady and relatively noiseless compared with my abode of the previous fortnight. Looking back, it was surprising how little rest I had been able to get, but I had not seemed to need as much sleep, probably because the whole period had been split into so many parts and the cattle completely unaware of normal 'office' hours.

One seemed to be able to draw on a boundless energy, which no doubt was generated by the total unpredictability of events and the excitement of a completely new environment. But now that it was all over, I could feel a great weariness creeping over me and, after bathing, changing and partaking heartily of a good meal, I decided that the armchair before the fire was the best antidote and an ideal way to spend my first evening at home.

I was awakened by a gentle nudging at my shoulder. 'Sorry, Hugh,' said Diana gently, 'but I've got a bit of a problem.' She motioned to the hallway. 'There are three little waifs at the door. They've walked up from Barton House. They're awfully upset – they say their dog is sick. Will you come and have a word with them . . . ?'

Despite my previous feeling of well-being, it was difficult not to feel a trifle grumpy at the request.

Diana sensed my reaction immediately, she was good at that: 'I know you're tired, dear,' she said, 'But I didn't have the heart to say you weren't in. They must have come all the way by themselves in the dark – poor little things. Just a quick word . . . there's a dear.'

So, wriggling my feet into my slippers and rubbing the sleep from my eyes, I followed her into the hall.

There were three of them, pale-faced and standing together in the light of the porch.

The eldest was a girl, tall and thin and aged about twelve. Her hair was short and roughly cut and she wore a green dress that was far too old for her, obviously designed for a small woman. Her jacket was shabby, a size too large, and could have been made for a boy; no socks or stockings, just a pair of dull blue court shoes with inch-high heels.

At her side stood a small boy, his face screwed up in a permanent frown, his haircut even rougher than the girl's; and his clothes, although slightly more well-fitting, had seen better days.

The third member of the forlorn little trio was a tiny girl, with long blonde hair to her shoulders, held back from her face with two enormous pink slides, one on each side of her forehead. Her hands were enveloped by the overlong sleeves of a grey cardigan which came down to her knees, just short of the hem of a faded tartan skirt.

But it was when she looked up that I could understand why Diana had had to fetch me, for though she made no sound, no sobbing or crying, the tears were streaming down her little face, their straggly tracks glistening in the reflected light.

Barton House was an old dwelling about a mile outside Ledingford, which the Council used to house destitute families. I had passed it on many occasions, but had never actually been inside.

The inhabitants were of mixed origin, with a proportion of travellers who used to 'come inside' for the winter. As a result, the forecourt of what had been in its day a quite imposing country dwelling, was littered with old caravans, car bodies, piles of scrap, lines of ragged washing, smouldering fires, dogs, cats, chickens and the occasional goat.

Yet, despite the initial impression of hopelessness, if

134

anything caught the attention it was the fun and games and general happiness of the tattered mob of kids who were ever-present.

They amused themselves with the most rudimentary objects: chair legs and bedsteads were constructed into obstacles over which tyreless bicycles were ridden. Old pram chassis, converted into 'chariots', were raced down the bare slopes at the back of the dwelling, while little girls played 'house', often conducting their juvenile chores in a far more orderly fashion than their feckless parents, who just sat, smoked and stared into space.

It used to remind me of lambing time, with the youngsters gambolling and merrymaking in the fields, whilst the old sheep just stood about, seemingly fed up that another spring had come round.

And now standing at my door, were three of those lambs from down at Barton House.

'Come inside,' said Diana. 'You must be frozen.'

The girl in the green frock reacted to my wife's offer with a start, just like a lamb or fawn that had suddenly found fear. She stood back a pace and, taking hold of the little ones, drew them closer to her.

'Come on,' Diana coaxed gently, holding out her hand as she spoke. At that, the boy took a step even further back, only to be yanked forward again.

'Come on, Frank. The lady won't 'urt yer,' admonished the tall girl, now regaining her confidence, and, as she spoke, the little one with the long blonde hair and tears took hold of Diana's hand and stepped inside.

'What's your name?' asked Di, kneeling in front of her.

'Luce,' came the sniffly response.

'Lucy! You're Lucy!' said the elder girl firmly. 'An' 'e's Frank, an' I'm Gloria, but they calls me Glory, an' I don' mind that. An' we'm from Barton House and our Pickles is sick ... an' we...' Tears welled up, almost instantaneously, in her wide eyes. 'We love 'er ... an' we don' know what to do...'

She looked away and, reluctant to let go of the hands of

her two charges, wiped her suddenly wet cheeks on the shoulder of her drab jacket.

I decided to wait a second or so before trying to obtain some further information about the symptoms, but then Frank involuntarily filled in the raw details.

'She got took by the dog when she was wantin',' he said, his face stern and still set in a deep frown. 'Now Nan says she's payin' for it!'

'Nan says?' I queried.

'Our Nana,' explained Glory, pulling Frank sharply by the arm before he could reply. 'She looks after us.'

'We ain't got no Mam,' blurted Frank, pulling his arm free.

Diana looked across at me; she, too, had tears in her eyes and suddenly I felt I had been there before.

Wayward bulls, loony cooks, inebriated Finns or the Baltic Sea in a Storm Force Ten were all tough numbers; but in Ledingford and my country practice there were simple, down-to-earth matters that were a darn'd sight more difficult to cope with.

'Can you help them, Hugh?' appealed Di.

'Yes, but I don't exactly know . . .'

'She's 'avin pups,' said Frank with a sigh, obviously not very impressed that he practically had to spell out the situation to someone whom he had been led to believe was an expert in such matters. ''Avin pups – an' Uncle Ned says she's "bound"!'

I was determined not to ask who or what Uncle Ned was, though Frank's eyes were glued to my face, ready for it.

Diana, Glory, Lucy and, of course, Frank were all waiting for my response. What could I say? I could not ring Bob Hacker or McBean with this one, tired though I was.

The enigma of veterinary practice! For the past fortnight I had been in charge of the health and welfare of about £200,000-worth of cattle – a big responsibility – and now . . . ? Only hours after the completion of my contract, here came an appeal – silent, tearful, rather pathetic – with not a lot of money at stake, if any, but presenting an equal responsibility. Just as for Captain Schwarz and Mr Mumme – big ships, or little ships such as *Dagmar Hansen* – from the professional they both demanded a similar dedication.

Weary though I was, I could not pass the buck.

'Just like the Windmill,' I said to Di.

'We never close,' she replied, smiling in answer to one of our stock jokes. 'I'll make some coffee. I expect you three could do with a warm drink, too.'

Glory attempted to decline the offer, saying she thought they should get back to Pickles as soon as possible. But Diana insisted and, after cocoa and biscuits for them and coffee for me, we set off in the car for Barton House.

The two girls sat in the back and, save for an occasional inaudible whisper from Lucy to her elder sister, remained silent. Frank, however, sat in the front beside me and, with a little prompting, proceeded, on a man-to-man basis, to give a potted history of their circumstances.

Their father was 'away' and it was not known when he would be back. They were looked after by Nana, their grandmother, and by Uncle Ned, who sounded like Nana's brother. The family had been moved to Barton House by the 'public', by which I assumed Frank meant the Council, from the Belbury district where they had lived in a van.

'That was nice,' said Glory, breaking the silence in the back. 'There was a big farm, an' apples an' hops, an' all lovely and green. Then Dad went away and Mam got ill with the baby.' She lapsed into silence once again. Remembering that Frank had earlier said they had no mother, I was intrigued to know what had happened, but could not bring myself to ask. And as no further information was forthcoming, I left it at that.

Shortly, we approached Barton House which, from a distance, appeared deceptively homely, with lights in most of the windows. The fact that a lot of them had broken panes, stuffed with rags or newspaper, was not evident at night, neither were the missing tiles or hanging gutters; it was only when one drew closer that the dilapidation and dereliction became evident.

Turning off the road, we jerked over the pot-holed track as far as possible; then the way became barred by an abandoned, battered pram, an old table on its back and a section of an iron bedstead, gleaming in the lights of the car.

I stopped and the children scrambled out and ran for the house, leaving me alone by the car. Up the broken steps they scampered, disappearing through the half-open door.

Looking about me, even in the darkness I decided Barton House had been a most attractive residence in its day. Red-bricked, as were many of the larger country houses built in the late 1800s, and well appointed for its time, although the acute pitch of the tiled roof, together with the arched windows and doorways, gave it a rather monastic air. The structure was solid, with window surrounds in dressed stone, whilst the upper storey had dormer windows at regular intervals. I could count at least eight chimney stacks, each with two or three chimneys, and surmised that the house must have possessed a considerable number of rooms. A baby crying, a man's voice calling, some saucepans rattling, a door slamming – sounds of somewhat subdued activity came to my ears. Then I heard a woman shouting in a voice that seemed to be Irish, although I could not be sure. Her outburst was followed by a high-pitched retort, which I did recognise – it was Glory. Then another door slammed, this time loudly. The woman shouted, 'You're a wicked girl, so y'are!' and I heard Glory shouting back, but could not make out what she was saying.

I was moving towards the steps when I caught sight of an old man standing in the doorway of the porch. He was bent, leaning on a stick, and dressed in chapel black, a tweed cap on his head and a white muffler about his neck. How long he had been watching me I could not tell and, as

I approached, he raised his stick and pointed it towards me.

'Are you the veterinary, now?' There was a faint Irish lilt in the way he spoke.

'Yes,' I said. 'Are you Uncle Ned?'

He lowered his stick and leaned upon it, a faint smile crossing his lined face. 'Told ye it all, have they? Little divils. Never said they were goin'. Didn' know where they was. Nan's bin frantic!'

It was then that I began to understand the apparently violent reception that Glory had encountered on her return. Who wouldn't give three young kids like that a wigging, for wandering off in the night?

'Worried about their dog,' I said, as if trying to excuse their action. 'What's the matter?'

'Belly full o' pups, an' can't get rid of 'em,' grunted the old man. 'Waters came this mornin'. All dead, I shouldn't wonder – an' that's no loss round 'ere. Too many mouths as it is!'

He was rambling on about the conditions at Barton House, when a light appeared in the passage behind. There was a shuffling, some footsteps; then a tall woman, her grey hair drawn back in a bun, appeared beside him. She wore a shawl about her shoulders, drawn over a woollen jumper, with a long black skirt to her ankles. Glory stood beside her, eyes full and tearful, but there was no sign of the other two. This, I guessed, was Nana.

'I'm sorry they troubled ye, sir,' she said, firmly. 'They had no right to do it, they didn't. But they're only children, sir. They don't know, ye see ... they don't.'

'Their dog's having trouble with the pups – they're naturally concerned,' I replied, looking across at Glory, who wiped her eyes and turned away.

'She'll be all right, sir,' said the woman.

'If she's been on since morning, she should have produced something by now,' I replied, sensing a degree of rising hostility.

'So she should!' It was Ned, coming to life again. 'So she

should!' he repeated, stamping his stick on the ground. 'Strainin' her heart out, since the early hours. She's in trouble all right!'

'Bide yer whisht!' the grey-haired woman snapped. 'She'll have to take her chance!'

'Let me look at her,' I suggested. 'See what it's all about.'

With that, the grandmother stepped down in front of the others and stood before me. Though her face was lined and drawn, her eyes were still clear and bright and she stood straight, with her shoulders back. A fine looking woman still, I thought; and, like Barton House, both had seen prouder days.

She confronted me squarely, but as I looked at her I noticed her face softening and, curling her lower lip, she bit it gently, as if stifling a degree of embarrassment – from what she said next, I had guessed right.

'We don't have a copper to spare, sir. To spend on dogs!'

So that was it. That was what had been responsible for the hostility. They were broke.

To me, that had been pretty obvious from the start.

'It's a bit cold, standing here,' I said, shrugging my shoulders. 'Can we go in and talk about it? There's no charge for that.'

'Oh! What am I thinkin' of, now?' she exclaimed, raising her hands to her face. 'Come in, sir. Come in. What must you think of me, keeping you outside the door like this?'

She turned, waving the children ahead of her, and motioned me to follow, which I did, leaving old Ned to shuffle along behind.

The passage-way was long and rather narrow. I caught sight of two other women and some children ahead, obviously interested in the 'goings on'. But we turned off before we got that far and entered a large, square, high-ceilinged room. A reasonable fire flickered in the grate, which seemed surprisingly small for the size of the room. Over the top of the mantelshelf, a large mirror with a gilt frame reflected the austerity of the surroundings, except where the damp had removed the 'silvering' from its face.

Part of the far end was curtained, behind which I glimpsed some beds and a wardrobe. But the centre-piece of the bed-sitting-living-room was a large, oblong table, set for a meal; and, although the crocks and cutlery were of an endless variety, they were clean and arranged in orderly fashion. I counted five places, which must have been for Nana, Ned and the three children. A kitchen cabinet, cream-coloured and a trifle rusty, stood beside a smaller table against one wall, next to an enamel sink. On the table there was a small electric cooker, some saucepans and other cooking utensils. Two armchairs, a sofa, a thinning carpet and a mahogany sideboard occupied the rest of the space – it was all a bit of a jumble, to say the least.

'Here she is!' Glory knelt down by an old eiderdown covered with a sheet, in the corner by the window, and stroked the little black and white Jack Russell. 'Vet's come to make you better, Picky,' she said gently, ruffling the bitch's ears.

'How old is she?' I asked, kneeling beside her.

'Mam got her for us. Christmas before last – she was ever so little and she nearly died then. But I looked after you, did'n I, Picky?' Glory leaned forward and put her head close to Pickles and the little terrier, in turn, raised its head as far as it was able and wagged its stumpy tail in appreciation.

'Let me have a look at her,' I said, and Glory eased back for me to get closer. It was obvious that Pickles was exhausted from her efforts; her abdomen was swollen and rock-hard, and below, her teats were full and dripping milk. Behind her, staining the sheet, was a copious green discharge, suggesting that, whilst the womb must be open, the passage of the pups was, for some reason, obstructed.

'I'd like to examine her internally,' I told Nana. 'Could I have some soap and warm water?' Then I explained to the children what I was going to do. They listened in silence, without showing any signs of surprise or emotion.

Gently inserting my finger into the birth canal, I probed

forward. As I did so, Pickles strained and groaned and Glory, without any prompting, stroked her pet's head and comforted her, whilst Lucy and Frank, hands in his trouser pockets, watched intently.

The canal was dry and narrow, although, as I had expected, the neck of the womb was well dilated. But I could feel no head, legs or even tail of a presented puppy, just a slightly ballooned structure, with a bony ridge running horizontally. It was the backbone of the first puppy, which was lying crossways, and all that Pickles' energetic contractions had achieved was to jam it tighter into the aperture – it was a real problem.

'Too big?' queried old Ned, from a chair by the fireside.

I made no comment, for I was trying with my index finger to rotate the obstructing pup's body – but it would not budge. Manipulation was out, I decided; there was only one solution: a caesarian!

Easing out of the vaginal passage, I sat back on my haunches and washed my hands in the adjacent bowl of water.

'Can you help her?' asked Nana, passing me a towel.

'A large puppy is lying sideways – only his back and spine are presented,' I explained. 'It's too tight to move, so there's only one solution. It will have to be a caesarian operation.'

Nana gasped audibly: 'An operation! Lord help us! We can't afford an operation!'

I was tired and could well have done without such a job. I suppose I could have given Pickles a relaxant, in the faint hope that by morning the offending pup would be in a better position and, if it was not, operate then. But that was another twelve hours away and far too long to leave things. As for charging for the work, well, if I did it now, it was in my own time and that way, although Bob Hacker was in any case pretty reasonable, there would be no respercussions in the practice, for it would just be the cost of materials. So, without trying to sound too saintly, I told Nana not to worry about the money.

'I'll take Pickles away with me to the surgery, and do the best I can for her,' I told them. 'It's the only way.'

The reaction stunned me.

Glory, who had been on her knees comforting Pickles, leaped to her feet like a spring uncoiling, her face white and her eyes wild. Her frail body appeared to go rigid and she clenched her fists with such force that the knuckles blanched immediately. Then she screamed at the top of her voice and came at me, flailing the air with her arms until she made contact with my chest, beating me furiously. 'You won't! You won't! You're not takin' her! You're not!' she cried, her voice shrill and frenzied. 'You're not 'avin 'er. Not to that 'ospital!'

I managed to take hold of her wrists, but for a spindly little girl she had amazing strength. Then Nana stepped forward and, grasping her firmly by the shoulders, pulled her away and shook her hard.

'Quiet! Quiet, girl! D'ye hear!' she shouted, turning Glory to face her. And Glory, still hysterically crying 'No! No!', put her arms tightly around her grandmother and buried her head in her woollen shawl. Lucy and Frank, white-faced and also on the verge of tears, had drifted over to Uncle Ned by the fire and were standing, holding on to his knees, one at either side.

Glory's unexpected outburst had shaken me as well. I felt confused and could not even clearly remember what I had said.

Nana's hands gently caressed the sobbing child's head, in an attempt to soothe and comfort her.

'They took her Mam for that, sir, d'ye see,' she said, quietly. 'Took 'er, an' she never come back.'

I looked over to Uncle Ned and the other two by the fire. He shook his head silently and put his arms round them.

It was a tragic situation and I felt deeply distressed by the circumstances – but there was no way round it. Pickles would not have her pups without an operation, so what was I to do?

I did another internal examination, but there was no

change: the jammed puppy was in exactly the same place as before.

'Why can't yer do it 'ere?' asked Ned. 'Seen a vet t'other side of Belbury do it on a sow once. Never took 'er to no surgery!'

I was about to put up the reasons against his suggestion, when it crossed my mind that if I went back to the surgery there would be no help, for Miss Billings was visiting her sister in Bradford. Diana could not come because she was looking after Sara, and I could not really get McBean or Bob Hacker out, if it was going to be for charity. The only problem was anaesthesia – I had no ether and was short on barbiturate – but I could narcotise with morphine sulphate and use local. It was a method I had seen C. J. Pink using with great success, when I saw practice with him as a student. As for the rest of the necessary equipment, my surgical case was complete and there was light, water and help available.

I put my hand on Glory's shoulder. She was quieter now, her little frame only occasionally jerking with a gentle sob.

'I won't take Pickles away,' I said, quietly, 'but she must have an operation. If you, Lucy and Frank will stay over there with your Uncle, and Nana will give me a hand, I'll do it here!'

Nana looked up, slightly startled. Then she regained her composure. 'All over a little scrap of a dog,' she said, blowing out her cheeks. Then she smiled. 'Sure an' I'll help you, sir. You're a saint so ye'are.'

It was a compliment that I felt was undeserved, although I did wonder whether the fact that St Francis of Assisi did not charge for his services either, had something to do with my sudden beatification.

It took twenty minutes to get it all set up. It transpired that there were two other rooms, where Nana and Ned slept, and Nana went off to one of them to fetch a sheet to cover the small table on which the cooker had stood: it was just the right height to operate on. Conveniently, it was next to the sink, but I needed extra light and fetched my hand-lamp from the car. Donning my red rubber apron, I explained the procedure to Nana, now divested of her shawl, her sleeves rolled up and sporting a blue pinafore. I pointed out the various instruments and what I was likely to ask her to hand me.

Lucy and Frank were ordered to sit on one of the beds, with the curtains drawn back, which they did without any question. Glory sat on Uncle Ned's knee, by the fire, biting her thumbnails nervously.

I had previously injected a quarter of a grain of morphine sulphate, in solution, under Pickles' skin and, by the time we were ready to commence, she was snoozing peacefully. Normally, morphine was best in combination with atropine to avoid excessive salivation, but as I had none, I was going to have to manage without it – but it did mean that I was going to have to keep an extra-special eye on her breathing.

Carefully, I lifted the little bitch onto the cooker table and gently laid her down, for even in such a soporific state, sudden shocks or noise can cause the patient to react violently. I tied her legs fore and aft with bandage to the drawer handles at either end, and then shaved the site, using Uncle Ned's razor. Finally, after cleaning and sterilising, I infiltrated the operating area and the deep muscles with Novocain.

When I was satisfied that it was completely numb and Pickles' colour good and her breathing steady, I glanced across to Nana who, though grim-faced, gave me a re-assuring nod; then I took the scalpel and made an incision through the skin.

About three inches long, in the lower third of the left flank, it ran parallel with the spine and about one and a half inches behind the costal arch. Such was the abdominal distension that I was able to appreciate the coiled left horn of the womb and make my entry directly over it.

On incising the skin and subcutaneous fat, I severed a few small blood vessels, but quickly ligated them, getting

145

Nana to trim off the loose ends of the ties. I passed on through the deeper muscles, ligating a few further vessels, through more fat, eventually reaching the transverse layer, the last muscle barrier before the peritoneum and the abdominal cavity. This was the tricky point, and I checked Pickles' respiration rate before proceeding any further. Now I had to incise over the expanded womb, without cutting it; the technique was to lift the lateral muscle with forceps and make an initial puncture with the point of the scalpel, then, inserting my flat, Mayo scissors, enlarge the opening safely.

It worked well, and when I had achieved entry I looked up at Nana and breathed a sigh of relief – but her face was set in deep concentration and she gave no reaction.

Beneath the aperture lay the pregnant womb and carefully I attempted to ease the nearest horn to the outside, in order that when I removed the first pup, the attendant fluids would not run back into the body cavity. But the organ was so distended that, in drawing it up, I feared it might tear, so I decided to pack it well and incise it where it was. Fixing the fleshy wall to the lip of the incision, I probed it with my finger, feeling for a recognisable extremity of the puppy inside. As part of the preparation, I had got Nana to prepare a hot water bottle, placing it beneath a sheet inside a cardboard box, to receive the newborn, and, before making the ultimate cut, I looked over my shoulder to check that it was handy. My eyes met Glory's, who had been standing at my elbow all the time. She gave a weak smile. 'All right?' I asked. She nodded. Then I continued my work.

When the first puppy came, it appeared lifeless. It was large, nearly all white except for a black patch on its left flank. I squeezed away the membranes and severed the cord, before placing it in some cotton-wool and handing it to Nan. 'Rub it gently,' I told her, hoping there was some life in it, for if this one at the back of the womb had not survived, there was little hope for the rest – and I did so want to get live pups.

Nana rubbed it and stroked it. 'Blow on its nostrils,' I told her. This she did, and the little creature opened its pink mouth and yawned – it was alive!

How the atmosphere altered. 'Let me see! Let me see!' shouted Glory excitedly, as Lucy and Frank, who could remain at a distance no longer, came close as well.

'Take it easy,' I cautioned. 'I don't want Mum to wake up just yet.' And I set to, to deliver the next.

There were five pups in all, each one alive, including the dog pup that had caused the obstruction, in itself a minor miracle. Everyone, including Ned, took turns in rubbing them and chattered excitedly about what they were going to call them, while I closed the wounds and sutured the muscle layers and skin.

The morphine worked out just right and, as the last stitch went in, Pickles raised her head, pricking her pointed ears at the squeaking of her new family in the cardboard box below.

I left Barton House just on two o'clock in the morning. Nana had made some cocoa as a nightcap, but I doubted very much if there would be any sleep in that house for a while. I had promised to call the following day, to see that Pickles was making a normal recovery, and was thankful to crawl into my own bed at last.

Diana awoke and wanted to know all about it. I told her about Glory's outburst and the reason she was so upset, and how the Caesar went.

'So much for my night off,' I said wearily, as I rolled over and closed my eyes.

'Worse things happen at sea,' said Diana, giving me a gentle dig in the ribs.

And, being too tired to disagree, I called it a day!

# 10

Doing jobs for 'charity' was not uncommon in the Hacker practice. Some, like Pickles' caesarian, were genuinely deserving of a philanthropic attitude; but there were others where the term 'charity' could not be so readily applied, though when it came to cash receipts the end result was often the same.

The offenders were known as 'slow-payers', their reluctance to part with their money on a monthly basis probably a relic of the days when debts were settled following the gathering of the corn at the end of the season. I was once firmly reminded of this when attempting, on practice instructions, to encourage a 'slow payer', one Arnold Barford, to settle more regularly. He eyed me for a while, like a great bull-frog contemplating a fly, then said:

'Young man, when you been around as long as I 'ave, you'll find out that the good Lord only intends us all to 'ave one 'arvest a year, no matter how 'ard we works!'

Another who was even more financially tardy was Grandad Berry; a bent and wizened little man permanently attired in a tattered, string-tied overcoat and an odd-shaped trilby hat. He lived with his large family at The Gockett, a rustic farmstead on the top of a hill from which he rarely descended. Over the years he had fathered two broods, for, following the death of his first wife, he had married his young housekeeper who, at the time, was not much older than his own children. Their joint offspring, being much younger, always referred to their father as 'Grandad', as in turn did everyone else.

My first visit to The Gockett was a memorable one on several counts; it was early in my career at Ledingford, at a time when geographically I was still becoming acclimatised. The call to a mare with colic was passed on to me by Bob Hacker, just after ten o'clock one Thursday night.

'Take the Billington road,' Bob had directed over the phone, 'and, after you go through the village, carry on for about two miles until you get to a junction. Take the left fork and, after another mile, there's a clump of beech trees on the right by a track running up through a wood. Continue up there until you come to the Keeper's Cottage; drive round the back of it and up the slope – you'll find a gate at the top. Through there, across two fields, and The Gockett is straight in front of you. Think you'll find it?'

It was a daft question, for Bob certainly did not expect me to say 'no' and the instructions, although somewhat copious, sounded reasonably straightforward.

'I should think so,' I said finally, jotting down the last direction on my pad.

'See if you can get some money out of him, too,' added Bob. 'Tell him this is a veterinary practice, not Lloyd's Bank!'

'I'll see what I can do,' I said, thinking to myself that Bob himself was the world's worst when it came to chastising clients about overdue accounts – a feature common amongst vets who, in the main, are not the best of businessmen.

It was one of Dylan Thomas's 'crow-black' nights, with the lights of my little Ford seeming to bounce back from the wall of darkness ahead. I drove through Billington, slumbering beneath the southern ridge of Bradstone Hill, and on towards The Gockett, positioned as it was atop the northern end.

With some difficulty, after reaching the fork, I eventually defined the clump of beeches, not easily apparent on such a night, and rattled off up the woodland path. At the Keeper's Cottage a lamp burned dimly behind the curtains; but my arrival which, due to the terrain and the roaring of my engine, produced a combination of sounds highly unlikely to go unnoticed, stimulated no outward activity. Aware of the racket I was creating, I swung wide of the house before rounding the back of it. 'Up the slope,' Bob had said, though, as I drove on, the ground did not appear to rise as steeply as I might have anticipated. However, the going was good so I kept pushing ahead.

I was surprised not to encounter any livestock, for the grass appeared very tightly grazed and, even in the lights of the car, looked green and in good heart. This seemed somewhat contrary to the impression of Grandad that Bob had given me, when he had run through a brief 'Who's Who' in the Hacker practice, some time previously.

'Dog and stick,' had been the description applied to the old man's standard of husbandry at the time, but from what I could see at that point, I had to admit that I found the cultivation of his pastureland most impressive.

I had not yet come to the promised gateway, although the gradient was starting to increase gradually, my rear wheels beginning to slip as the ground became softer.

Then suddenly, it steepened considerably and I found getting a grip almost impossible. I made several attempts, taking a different line for each assault; finally I was successful and, after mounting the ridge, stopped and got out of the car to take my bearings.

It was like standing with one's head up a chimney-piece – soot-black and silent; not a sound to be heard or a star to be seen. I walked to the front of my little Ford, the wheels now encased in thick red mud as a result of clawing its way up the bank. In the lights I could see that the going ahead was quite level, and I was about to get back into the driving seat when a fluttering shape passed briefly across my eyeline. I thought at first it was an owl on the wing, but when it appeared again I took a few paces forward to investigate.

I came upon a flag, a yellow triangular flag on a pole. Printed upon it was a number – six. And it stood in a small, metal-rimmed hole. Suddenly my position became clear – no wonder the grass was tight and in good heart. I was not on a cow pasture at all – I was on a bloody golf course!

I looked back at my mud-covered wheels and realised that the approach to the green would most certainly be labelled 'Ground under repair' after my passage, but thankfully the sacred sixth itself had been spared and the members saved from a communal fit of apoplexy.

So that night marked not only my first visit to Grandad Berry, whose access I had missed by not turning tight enough at the Keeper's Cottage, but my first visit to Moresley Golf Club. A few years later I became a member myself, and often had a secret smile when putting on the sixth or standing on the tee and remembering my first 'drive' up that fairway.


I finally arrived at The Gockett. No comment was made on my delayed arrival, so I did not mention the unexpected detour I had taken and made ready for my examination of Grandad Berry's old skewbald mare, Mary.

After scooting away a little band of juvenile onlookers, who should in my opinion have all been long abed, the old man closed the stable door, placing a lighted Tilly on each of the low window ledges at either side.

'Where's Mr Hacker?' he asked suspiciously. 'He do come, mostly.'

'His night off,' I told him, patting Mary gently on the flanks. 'I'm Hugh Lasgarn, his assistant.'

'Knows about 'orses, do yer?'

'Yes,' I said, without looking back and, taking my stethoscope, started listening to Mary's bowel sounds.

I gave her a thorough check; she was an old lady, her teeth quite worn and, from the quality of the fodder that was on offer, I concluded she was suffering from impaction – constipation of the large gut.

An internal examination revealed the contents to be as solid as concrete; I cleared what I could but there was obviously more to come. It was a case for what the old books described as a 'drastic purge', and when Grandad described the concoction he had already poured down

Mary's throat to no effect – Glauber's Salt, castor-oil, mustard seeds and ginger – I decided that 'drastic' was a very descriptive term.

'She's pretty stopped,' I said.

'You save 'er, Mr Lasgarn,' said Grandad. 'Loves that old mare more than both my missus put together, I do. You save 'er an I'll give yer anything!'

'Bit off your account would help,' I countered, remembering Bob's request.

'Ah!' said Grandad, pushing back his trilby. 'Yes, I must do that. Only fair to do that. You save Mary an' you shall 'ave your money.'

That, I thought, was a deal – and to go back to the practice with Grandad's cash in my hand would stand me in good stead for the pay rise that I had been promised after my first three months.

'You're on, Grandad,' I said, using his title automatically, and opened up my case.

I was intending to use a drug called Carbachol. I had heard about its reputation in impactive colic, though as yet had never had the opportunity to use it; now was my chance!

There was one factor that invoked a degree of caution with its use – to eliminate the possibility of a twist in the gut – for the action of Carbachol was to stimulate smooth muscle contraction. This in turn activated the bowel, expelling the contents; but if a twist was present the drug only served to aggravate the condition. However, the symptoms of a twisted gut were far more positive in the early stages and I was confident that Mary was not suffering from that condition.

As I prepared the syringe, Grandad looked on suspiciously.

'This new, then?' he enquired.

'No,' I said.

'Never seen no injections for this job afore. Mr Hacker allus tubes 'er.'

'I think the old lady has had enough liquid down her throat,' I told him. 'This is more scientific.'

'Oh aye. Scientific,' said Grandad noncommittally as he rubbed his whiskery chin. 'Well, you knows – you'm the expert!'

At that early stage in my career, I was quite pleased by his remark, regarding it as a compliment and not understanding that the true interpretation was, 'I hope you know what you're doing!'

To be honest, I was just feeling my way with the case, for my experience of colics so far had been of the spasmodic type, which responded to sedation;' Mary was my first impactive case.

The stable was quite small, accommodating just the one animal, with the manger at the head and the half-door flanked by two large-paned windows at each side.

'Bring the light round here,' I ordered. 'The drug's got to go into her neck.'

Grandad obliged, steadying Mary's head with his free hand, while I gently injected the contents of the syringe.

''Ow long do it take?' he enquired.

'Not long,' I said, but as it was the first time I had used it, I could not be sure, though the instructions had indicated the action was 'rapid and intense'. I took the Tilly from him and held it up so that I could observe the response more closely.

Mary first laid her ears back, then turned to observe her right flank, indicating something was on the move inside, but she looked away again as if it was a false alarm. A minute or so later she started picking up her feet uneasily.

'Untie her, in case she goes down,' I suggested. But she did not go down; instead, she broke out into a sweat, the moisture glistening in narrow streaks on the darker parts of her coat.

'Is 'er goin' to be all right?' questioned Grandad anxiously.

'Yes,' I said, fingers crossed. 'Just give it time.' As I spoke, Mary's flanks started to heave and she groaned lengthily. 'It's working,' I said enthusiastically.

But five minutes later nothing further had happened.

'You better tube 'er,' said Grandad. 'That science of your'n ain't going to work!'

'Just give it a little longer,' I said.

'Don' want to lose 'er,' said Grandad. Neither did I, but with the Carbachol not seeming to be effective, I was not at all confident about any other form of treatment and, apart from the 'no cure – no fee' arrangement, my reputation as a 'horse vet' was at stake as well. However, the stomach tube it would have to be.

'I'll need to make up the mixture,' I told him, after giving the drug a further five minutes to act. 'Can I have some more warm water?'

'Better come to the 'ouse,' he said. 'Science, be damned!'

But no sooner had the words left his lips than there came a sound like a distant whistle, that gradually filled in depth and volume until it reached the richness and profundity of a mighty bassoon. Mary shivered, gave a high-pitched whinny and raised her tail.

What followed, apart from the loudest fart I had ever heard in my life, was quite remarkable: accompanied by a shock wave as generated by a gigantic firework, the air became filled with flying missiles.

About the size of a man's fist and with the consistency of cannon-balls, they hurtled in all directions as the Carbachol finally produced results, aided in its ferocity, no doubt, by Grandad's concoction. Both he and I were unmercifully peppered by the objects as Mary, with unbridled relief, sprayed them all about.

One Tilly was knocked to the floor, smashing the globe, and, in rescuing it, Grandad got a clout in the eye. My case was bowled over and, finally, to the sound of splintering glass, Mary concluded her aerial display by breaking one of the windows!

'Told you it would work!' I said gleefully, as the old mare, with a satisfied look on her face, gave a huge sigh and started to nibble some hay.

When he had recovered from the unexpected assault,

Grandad picked up the undamaged lamp and held it aloft, slowly shining it around the stable, the rays finally resting on the shattered window.

'Aye. Better she is, all right,' he agreed.

'You'll settle your account, then?'

Grandad held up the light closely between us. 'What about the deductions?' he said.

'Deductions?'

'For the busted Tilly and the window. I'll reckon by the time I took for them, this job'll be about square! You see what Mr Hacker says when you do get back, then I'll let you 'ave the rest, next time. Eh?'

The old varmint's features settled into a grin that would have done Shylock proud and, despite my protestations, I came away that night from The Gockett empty-handed.

However, as I drove back to my digs, I decided there were, after all, some consolations: the treatment had worked and I was now more than familiar with the physiological properties of Carbachol, together with the fact that I also knew exactly where Moresley golf course was situated.

And as to golf, there was a feature in the game known as a 'stymie' which, thanks to Grandad Berry and Mary, I had learnt could also occur in situations other than on the putting green.

\* \* \*

Those were formative days, and folks like Grandad Berry were very much part of the communal richness of the Border Country.

As well as finding my way about in those early months, I was getting to know more and more clients. There was no better occasion to meet a fair cross-section of them, than at a funeral. In fact, the next time I was to come across Grandad was on the day they buried his near neighbour, Tom Glossop.

Country funerals were always well attended and, if Bob

Hacker was unable to represent the practice, either McBean or myself went along.

There, in the company of neighbouring farmers, agricultural workers, local gentry, auctioneers, keepers, Farmer's Union officials and corn merchants, the deceased were returned to the soil they had tended and, in turn, benefited from, during their allotted span.

There was quite a spate of such occasions following my arrival in Ledingford; not I may hasten to add, in any way connected with my presence, but I attended more funerals in the first three months of practice than I had ever done in my life, and some were highly unusual.

At the very first I went to, the undertaker himself collapsed with a heart attack and they rushed him to the cottage hospital in the back of his empty hearse; then there was a hop farmer who had left instructions for a small keg of beer to be buried alongside him, in case he finished up at the warmer of the two destinations, where a swig would come in handy!

Set amid the rolling countryside, the services never seemed clouded in melancholy: whether they were held at small grey-stone, mould-damp churches or at austere tin tabernacles, if the passing was the culmination of a full and industrious life, as the majority were, one could derive a degree of real satisfaction just from being present.

Perhaps my origins had something to do with it, for nobody loves a funeral more than the Welsh. Often, at the point of interment, as the mourners stood about, silent and bareheaded – solid, full-featured men, clasping their able hands before them, with their tweed-suited wives standing dutifully alongside – I would cast my gaze over the surrounding landscape.

In rain or shine, it looked so gently rich and fertile: the greens, the reds and golds of the fields, the cattle grazing, the river wandering slowly to the sea.

'In death there is life,' said the Good Book, and to me, standing silently amongst the Border folk in a country churchyard, it was easy to understand the reasoning.

Of course, country funerals were one of the accepted rural gatherings. A time to meet with neighbours and have a chat, and to some, like Grandad, who rarely socialised on any other occasion, to take advantage of the chance of communication.

Tom Glossop's funeral was just like that.

It was a wild and windy day in late summer. The rains had filled the crops, the sun had ripened them and now, as the gusts whirled the dusty traces of the combines high into the sky and taunted the apple trees to part early with their fruit, they laid old Tom to rest.

I was standing at the rear of the scattered crowd as the vicar said his words, when someone shuffled awkwardly to my side. Turning slowly and reverently, as one does on such occasions, I discovered to my surprise that it was Grandad. He must have moved quickly, because at the start of the graveside ceremony, just a few moments previously, I had spied him standing opposite me, behind the family mourners.

I gave a silent greeting which he acknowledged with a nod, the wind teasing his few remaining wisps of hair to stand vertically upon his head. As I turned again to face the ceremony, he moved a step closer.

'Mr Lasgarn!'

It was an abortive attempt at a whisper, coming across as a hiss and even more audible than if he had spoken normally.

'Mr Lasgarn!' he repeated, equally loudly. 'Could you do something for me?'

I half-turned towards him; he was breathing quite heavily and I thought perhaps he was feeling unwell and wanted help.

'Yes!' I said. 'Certainly! What can I do?'

He cleared his throat with a subdued cough, then, in another wheeze that all around could hear, flabbergasted me by saying:

'Could you come and cut a couple of pigs next Tuesday!'

Despite such rustic eccentricities, one could easily warm to country characters like Grandad, even though there were times when their apparent simplicity was questionable. These were the odd occasions when they 'tried it on', and an insurance claim for cattle struck by lightning was one of them.

Indeed, the next barney I had with Grandad was over exactly such a case, two cases in fact, and both were not without their element of intrigue.

The first followed a particularly violent storm at the time of the Three Counties Show which, for the first time, was being held at its permanent site at Malvern, after previously being held annually in turn at Hereford, Gloucester and Worcester.

The storm broke quite suddenly as Diana and I were driving over. Approaching British Camp, a jagged chain of brilliant white light sparked from the brooding cloud mass above; the ear-splitting crack and accompanying rumble that followed, seeming to shake the old Roman earthworks to its foundation.

'I hate thunder storms,' said Diana. 'Will it go away, do you think?'

'Looks more likely to be coming with us,' I said.

My observation, though perhaps somewhat tactless, was correct; however, it was not just the showground, but the whole of the three counties that were in for a battering.

Apart from being preceded by a few blisteringly hot days, there had been little indication of what was to come, but as we drove into the car park the first fat globs of rain hit the screen and ominously signalled the forthcoming weather pattern. As I switched off the engine, another white electrical streak fractured the sky, its attendant deep roar filling the air.

An inky cloud developed overhead and, with a fearsome rushing sound, there came a great wind, ragging the tents and banners, tearing at the blossom and gatecrashing the calm of the summer's day with wild indifference. Di and I sat, cocooned in the little steamed-up Ford, my arm around her until the eye of the storm had drifted on into mid-Worcestershire.

In its wake, to everyone's relief, came a fresh brightness that eased the tension instantly.

The showground had survived quite well, considering the downpour, and the newly laid concrete pathways made access free from mud; but in the surrounding countryside it was a different tale and the damage caused was extensive. Apart from the laying of corn and stripping of fruit by the tempestuous winds, the livestock had suffered, too, and we had several cases of death through suspected lightning stroke to investigate.

On of these was at The Gockett, home of Grandad Berry.

Insurance companies only pay out in such cases on verification of the cause of death as certified by a veterinary surgeon. The diagnosis in cattle is, in the main, circumstantial, such as the obvious one of there being a storm in the vicinity and the proximity of conducting material such as trees or metal in the form of barbed wire, troughs or railings. Limpness of the carcase without proper rigor and imperfect clotting of the blood are other indications, but are very subjective and actual burn marks very rare indeed.

With such variable parameters, it is not surprising that sometimes attempts are made to 'help things along', as I had first discovered some time previously, not at Grandad's, but from a not dissimilar country character called Mr Moon, who was making a claim for an aged Jersey cow.

There had been rain the previous night, but no thunder that anyone was aware of – except Mr Moon who affirmed vigorously that he had distinctly heard a resounding clap over his smallholding just before dawn. On arrival, I found the old cow lying in the yard and was instantly taken aback by the sight; for running from the tip of her right ear, down her shoulder, foreleg and onto her hoof was a bold singe mark – an obvious case of lightning and no need to look any further.

The fact that Mr Moon was a pipe smoker did not register with me at the time and I told Bob Hacker back at the surgery how simple it had been to make a diagnosis.

'Looked just as if someone had taken a lighter and run it from ear to toe,' I remarked.

'Is that so?' said Bob, pushing his chair back from the desk onto its back legs. 'Ever seen Joe Moon light his pipe?' He grinned. 'You just take a look next time you're there.'

And I did, as he opened a great brass lighter and, with a flick of the thumb, created a tall bright flame which instantly sent up clouds of acrid smoke from his curly tobacco.

'Carried him all through the war,' he said, when he noticed the attention I had been paying to it. 'You'd be surprised, yer would, Mr Lasgarn, what yer can set afire to with this,' he added with a broad wink.

A comment and a gesture that I well and truly noted for future reference.

Indeed, there were various tricks, and 'spoofing' the vet when it came to such enquiries was regarded in many quarters as fair play, rather than anything more devious.

Grandad Berry was one who knew a thing or two when it came to such matters.

At his request I arrived, this time by the approved route, and was led to the field where the incident had occurred. It was a fairly uneven pasture of about three acres, and considerably lush for the time of year.

The victim was a cross-bred yearling bullock, blown up like a drum.

'Struck the best beast on the place, right under this ere' ash,' said Grandad. '"Mind the Ash, 'e courts the flash!" You 'eard than un, ain't yer?'

This type of statement was the normal preface to most lightning examinations, communicating from the very beginning that there was really no doubt about the cause of death or the value of the victim.

However, uninfluenced, I commenced my examination. The symptoms were, as usual, rather vague; I stained a slide for anthrax, but found it negative for the bacilli, as I might have expected – though ever since missing a case and getting carpeted by the Ministry for it, I was particularly vigilant on that point.

Finally, I opened up the carcase to eliminate any other causes. The stomach was full of frothy gas and, with the lushness of the pasture, 'bloat' might well have the answer, though it had been a mighty storm and ash trees, as•Grandad had rightly commented, were about the most susceptible.

In my opinion, lightning was a reasonable diagnosis to make and I was on the point of telling Grandad I would fill in the form accordingly, when my eye caught a swathe of grass behind where the carcase lay, the blades flattened.

It looked as if something had been dragged across it.

Without making any comment, I followed the trail across the field to where quite a large area of grass appeared to have been compressed and a few specks of blood were spattered about.

'You're sure you found this beast under the ash?' I asked him.

Grandad frowned: 'What d'ye mean?' he said, trying to affect a disarming smile which did not quite work.

'Well, unless it was struck here, staggered over there, fell down and dragged itself back – how do you explain that grass?' I enquired.

Grandad shook his head in a mystified fashion; then suddenly his eyes lit up:

'Them boys!' he said. 'Them boys been a larking about!'

'What about the blood on the grass?' I persisted.

'Ah! Well! They larks pretty 'ard, do them boys, Mr Lasgarn,' he said. 'Pretty 'ard they do, an' that's for sure!'

I gave him lightning, though had I found the beast where I think he had dragged it from, I would possibly have put it down to 'frothy bloat' as it was lying in an open space and far away from any conducting agent. No doubt Grandad, the old varmint, was equally aware of that, too.

I was therefore somewhat surprised when he called me

back three days later to examine his best ram, which he also insisted had succumbed to the same fate during the storm, but this time the animal was lying dead on a roughly cultivated potato patch, situated on a mound that had the appearance of an ancient fort.

Three days lying in the sun had caused decomposition to set in, making a diagnosis of any sort not only objectionable, but extremely difficult – another trick of the trade, letting them cook a bit before ringing up!

'How come you didn't miss him until now?' I queried.

'Never thought to look on this patch. 'E must 'ave broke through the hedge over yonder.'

Sure enough, there was a gap in the distant boundary, some of the strong struts of blackthorn carrying strands of fresh wool.

It was impossible to tell, though around the neck there were dark marks that could have been discoloured by a strike – yet there were no conducting agents anywhere near.

Knowing what he knew, why had he not put it back in the hedge? That could have made the possibility a mite more likely.

'Bit rotten ter tell much,' said Grandad, agreeably.

With that I concurred. 'Pity there wasn't an ash tree or a bit of metal about,' I said, looking him straight in the eye. 'Would make a diagnosis easier, wouldn't it?'

'B'ain't no ash up 'ere,' he said, 'but metal, now. There could be some of that about. This patch up 'ere used to be a battle ground when them Normans was about these parts; must be a ton of metal hereabouts from their armour an' swords an' the like.'

Now that was a real try, though a bit too wild, even for him: 'You find me some and I'll believe you,' I said, smiling at his nerve.

'I'll get me spade,' he said. 'Left 'im up ere when I was doing some post 'oles.'

The ready presence of the tool sparked off a slight feeling of misgiving – then again, I thought, perhaps I was becoming overly mistrustful.

'Now where would yer like me to dig?' he asked.

'Well, if it's likely to be a conducting agent, it's got to be close to the sheep, hasn't it?' I suggested.

'Right yer be,' he puffed, and drove the blade into the soil right next to the carcase.

He tried three spots, and I was about to propose that he give up, when his spade grated on something solid. 'Now what 'ave we 'ere?' he said, pulling the object from the ground and handing it to me.

'Well, it isn't a spearhead,' I said. 'It's an old plough point.'

'Metal, ain't it?' he said, with a grin. 'That could 'ave done it. Eh?' So it was, and sufficient to be a conducting agent; unable to confirm any other cause of death, I agreed.

It was only on the way back down to Ledingford that I wondered if the ram had got hung up on the hedge and choked and Grandad had carried it across to the doctored patch – a bit farfetched I thought, I certainly was growing mistrustful. At the first incident, it was obvious that he had dragged the carcase, but in the ram's case there was no evidence of any disturbance to the land – not even any sheep's footprints!

If there were no footprints on the ground, which must have been softened by the rain storm at the time, then how on earth did it get there? My theory might not have been so wide of the mark, after all.

I decided not to complicate the issue any more. I had given him the benefit of the doubt in both cases – and why not?


A few years later I was to remember the incidents again, when Grandad passed away: his interment, at which I was present, was accompanied by a violent thunderstorm.

Perhaps 'Someone' knew the truth, but I was sure that of anyone, Grandad Berry would have a good explanation when he arrived at the 'other side'.

# 11

Probably one of the most essential prerequisites of any veterinary surgeon is the ability to communicate, not only with his patients, but with their owners as well, a factor which sometimes only serves to complicate matters even further.

Whilst it is often said that vets have a more difficult task in arriving at a diagnosis than doctors, because their patients are unable to offer any verbal description of the symptoms, Dr Brown, our family doctor, had other ideas.

'In that respect you are most fortunate, Hugh,' he once told me. 'The amount of irrelevant twaddle that some of my patients talk in the surgery is beyond belief.' Something in fact that was well demonstrated by old Mr Flack, following a consultation with me about his long-suffering spaniel dog, Jack.

Mr Flack and Jack were regular visitors to St Mark's Square and always posed a degree of difficulty, for Mr Flack was very deaf – his affliction, I often thought, being aggravated by a large hearing-aid that constantly emitted a low-pitched buzz, not unlike a bumble bee. The volume of this peculiar noise would gradually increase in intensity until, at a certain pitch, Jack would bark and old Flack would thump his chest at the spot where the aid was positioned beneath his pullover.

For a few seconds the old man, his spaniel dog and I would stand silent and motionless, waiting apprehensively to ascertain whether the bumble bee had been banished. If it had, the consultation would continue, but if it returned, Jack barked again and old Flack thumped his chest until success was achieved.

However, even with the instrument performing at maximum efficiency, it was still necessary to repeat, at least four times, any statement of importance if one wanted to ensure the old man got it right.

Otherwise, if, for example, I said, 'Mind how you go,' he would interpret it as, 'You think it's goin' to snow?' Or if I gave him some pills for Jack and said, 'Three times a day,' he was quite likely to think I was asking for money and would retort sharply, 'Of course I'm going to pay!'

Jack's problems were those not uncommon to Springers, such as infected ears, mild eczema and occasional stomach upsets, but more often than not, half the consultation would be taken up by Mr Flack asking my opinion of his own ailments, his wheezing chest, rheumatics or chilblains.

During this part of our conversation, I never repeated my responses more than once: it was hard enough to get the treatment for Jack correctly into his mind, and quadrupling up on any other matters would have taken up half of the morning.

It was this feature of the consultation that led Doctor Brown to call me one day.

'Hugh,' he said, 'I wonder can you enlighten me. I've got old Mr Flack here complaining that he's got 'cat's rash' – said you had diagnosed it. He's carrying on and wants to know where he's got it from, says he's never had a rash in his life and, what's more, he's never kept a cat either.'

I could not immediately follow Dr Brown and cast my mind back to the last time old Flack had been in my surgery. What on earth had I said to him?

'I've heard of "cat scratch fever" and allergic reactions, but this is a new one on me,' he added.

'Cat's rash'! It was a new one on me, too.

'I certainly didn't tell him that,' I said. 'Last time he was in, Jack was lame, a bit of arthritis – the old dog's getting on as well as Mr Flack. We talked about ageing – and we talked about loss of vision. And of course – ' then all became clear. 'We talked about CATARACTS!'

I heard Dr Brown chuckling on the other end of the phone. 'I was just beginning to wonder if you young vets were trying to take over the medical profession as well. Mind you,' he added, 'there's one or two of mine I wouldn't mind you having at all!'

Then there was the time I nearly got involved in a national crisis, again through not communicating clearly and precisely, over the condition of a tortoiseshell cat called Bertha. She had been neutered and, following the operation, which had been completely successful, had developed slight eruptions over various parts of her skin, a condition at that time thought to be a result of the change in hormone balance. The condition was considerably irritant to Bertha, who had scratched the offending areas so much that there were several bald patches in her coat, giving her a decidedly scruffy appearance.

Her owner, a Mrs Clift, was a lady of nervous disposition who reacted disconcertingly, with short agitated gasps, when I handled her pet, as if every move I made was causing undue pain.

I explained the possible causes of Bertha's ailment and suggested that a reduction in protein might be beneficial. 'We call it miliary eczema,' I concluded.

Mrs Clift's eyes popped. 'Oh dear!' she exclaimed, looking about her like a startled rabbit. 'Whatever will Alf say!'

Alf, of course, was Mrs Clift's husband and I was to find out what he said that evening.

In a voice that sounded like a foghorn with laryngitis, he announced over the phone who he was, then launched into a veritable tirade concerning Bertha, my diagnosis and, unbelievably, the responsibilities of the War Department!

'I wants papers from you in writing as to 'er condition!' he roared. 'They'll not get away with this! A cat can't help it if it goes under the fence, and what about us, me an' the missus? What if we catch it, eh?'

'Catch what?' I asked, genuinely confused by his outburst.

'That Military Eczema, of course! We was 'ere before that camp, an' if we suffers or anything 'appens to that cat, my God, they'll pay for it! Sure as my name is Alfred Clift!'

'Military Eczema?'

'That's what you said our Bertha'd got, didn't yer? And there's only one place she'd pick that up, an' that's that camp. An' I'm goin' to take this a lot further, so you just get those papers done up and . . .'

As Mr Clift fired on, I shook my head in disbelief. Miss Billings, our receptionist who was just leaving the surgery at the time I took the call, looked at me with concern.

'It's all right,' I said, putting my hand over the mouth-piece. 'Mr Clift's garden backs onto Pegton Army Camp and he thinks his cat's caught 'Military Eczema!'

I expected Miss Billings to burst out laughing, but instead her face assumed a look of absolute disgust. 'Poor creature!' she said. 'How dreadful. Dirty filthy soldiers, I never did like them!'

As for Mr Clift, I don't think he was ever really con-vinced by my explanation, muttering that I had changed my story and was probably in the pay of the Government and party to a 'cover-up'.

However, I eventually defused him and, though I waited over the next few days for a further salvo, his powder must have got damp for I never heard from him again.

When it came to explosive situations, probably the biggest dynamite brick I dropped, however, was in my very early days in practice, in the company of McBean at an agricul-tural function.

To begin at the beginning. One of the largest and most modern dairy farms in the County was owned by Lancelot Grangemouth, a very prosperous and highly respected personage, but a bit of a 'wet' with it.

His herd comprised over one hundred and fifty pedigree Dairy Friesians, grazed on extensive pasture and housed in winter in custom-built buildings. The parlour was of the new 'herring-bone' design, with automatic feeders and milking machines. A staff of four looked after the cows: the Head Cowman, Jack; Edgar and Phil, his aides, and a young lad, Colin, who was a general hand.

One of my first visits there was to investigate a case of infertility in one of the top milkers.

On arrival, I could find no one about and took the opportunity to make a complete 'recce' of the outfit. It certainly was most impressive and I was particularly fascinated with the automatic, hydraulic-release gates and cattle-handling facilities.

The office, which was unique for most dairy holdings at that time, was positioned alongside the parlour, its wall plastered with charts and graphs of milk averages, quality figures, feed conversions and calving intervals.

I was trying to decipher some of the tabulations when I heard a voice calling in the yard – it was Edgar who had noticed the car and guessed I was the new vet.

Edgar was in his sixties, one of the old school: flat-capped, heavily jacketed, his moleskins tucked inside turned-down, black wellington boots, and a man of few words.

He introduced himself briefly and led me to the cow, and as he tied her up for the examination, I tried to obtain some history concerning the case.

'Can you tell me anything about her?' I asked.

'Raving nympho!' said Edgar bluntly. 'If she ain't ridin' summat, they be ridin' 'er!'

It was a crude but fair description of a cow with cystic ovaries and, on further investigation, the diagnosis was supported by the position of the subject's tailhead, which was cocked upwards, a direct result of the excess oestrogen in the system slackening the ligaments that held it, and a recognised syndrome.

'Raised tailhead,' I remarked to Edgar.

'Arse in the air, more like!' he grunted.

Confining any further conversation to the bare essentials, I examined the patient internally to discover a cyst the size of a goose egg on her left ovary. It ruptured spontaneously and, after giving an intramuscular injection, I explained to Edgar how she should return to normal cycling and when would be the most likely time for her to conceive.

'You better put all that down in the book,' said Edgar. 'All got to be put in the book on this place, these days. Everything yer does – even got to write down 'ow many times yer drops yer pants!' He spat forcibly upon the straw. 'I'll show yer where it be,' he said and led off.

Edgar, I gathered, was not a happy man.

The book was a large ledger with a veterinary section, kept in a drawer in the office. I noted how Bob Hacker and McBean had recorded their entries and signed them: they were brief and to the point, so I commenced to do likewise.

'Damn! Didn't take her number,' I said. 'Do you know it, Edgar?'

'All numbers,' he muttered. 'No, I don't. You just put Sybil – they'll know 'er.'

The only available biro was rather leaky and dispensed the ink broadly, so, in bold blue letters, I wrote:

SYBIL – NYMPHOMANIAC. EXPRESSED AND INJECTED

Now that should have been the end of the story – and it would have been no bad thing if it had. However, the incident was revived in a most embarrassing fashion at the Ledingford Agricultural Club Dinner, a quite prestigious affair where the more 'County' farmers met once a month to discuss agricultural matters.

I had been invited as a guest of McBean who was a member, and found the evening most enjoyable, with excellent fare and no small quantity of wine to supplement it.

After dinner, the guests and members mingled, accompanied by more drinks and jovial chat, and McBean took the opportunity of introducing me to some of the clients who were present.

'Ah! Mr Grangemouth, sir!' Mac announced, addressing a tall man of somewhat military bearing, who turned about and looked down at us with a rather disinterested gaze; eyes half-closed and mouth pursed, accentuating a distinctly receding chin. 'Like to introduce Hugh Lasgarn, he's working with us.'

Lancelot Grangemouth nodded in my direction. 'Hyde-doo,' he mumbled. I held out my hand and he reciprocated half-heartedly with a 'wet fish' of a shake.

'Been to my place?' he asked.

Although his name immediately rung a bell, I could not instantly bring to mind the location of his farm which, considering the hospitality, was in some respects understandable. I racked my brains to remember – then suddenly it came: *'Sybil the nymphomaniac! She's yours!'*

Grangemouth's drooping eyelids shot up like spring-loaded blinds and his chin receded even further.

'McBean!' he exclaimed, looking furiously at my colleague.

'Hugh!' said McBean, looking at me.

*'Sybil. The old cow!'* I continued. *'The raving nympho!'*

'My cows don't have names!' retorted Grangemouth.

*'But I was told everybody knew Sybil!'*

*'So they might!'* he thundered. *'So they might! And I know her best of all – SHE'S MY WIFE!'*

I doubt if the Ledingford Agricultural Club ever had such an enjoyable evening, for the whole gathering was fully aware of the incident and many of them, catching it slightly out of context, took away with them the juiciest of tales to tell their respective spouses.

Further explanation pacified Grangemouth, though I felt not completely. McBean, however, could hardly contain his mirth.

'Ah, Hugh me boy,' he chuckled. 'You'll never know how near the mark ye were!'

'God! I could lose you a client over a thing like that, Mac,' I apologised.

'Don't worry your head. The way old Lancelot enjoys his lubrication, he'll not remember a thing in the morning.'

'As long as he doesn't read the book!' I added.

'The book?'

'The farm record book, veterinary section,' I explained.

And when I told him what I had written in there, even McBean did not think it was quite so funny!

Not all the misinterpretations were of my making, however, and more than once the proverbial boot was on the other foot.

There was the Irishman who, after setting his small shaggy terrier upon the examination table, very confidentially informed me that his pet was having trouble with his 'toot'!

I had a slight degree of difficulty explaining why I was feeling about the little dog's nether regions to obtain a diagnosis, after his owner further explained that the 'toot' was in his mouth – to be precise, an infected molar.

Nevertheless, the small animal clinics at St Mark's Square were flourishing and, in an attempt to avoid such problems recurring, I had instructed Miss Billings – who was responsible for the card index system I had devised – to obtain as much case history as possible, then fill me in with the details briefly, before the client came into the consulting room.

On most occasions she was very efficient, but sometimes, when, as McBean used to say, 'her moon was in the wrong quarter', she could be rather awkward. Then she would just march in, slap the card on the table and say: 'Thompson – ears!' or 'Fletcher – cough!'

Not, indeed, a lot to go on!

Her 'moon' had been disorientated for some few days and I was beginning to get a trifle annoyed with her attitude, so I asked her, very politely, if she would kindly try and give me a little more information about the cases than she had recently been providing.

Only those who have experienced the task of 'advising' a middle-aged spinster lady who has betrothed herself to a particular cause, albeit a veterinary practice, that her standard of performance is below par, will understand my difficulty.

Miss Billings gave one of her 'shakes', like a prize-winning turkey adjusting its feathers, pursed her lips and told me that diagnosis was my job, that she was only the 'book-keeper', and if I had any complaints about her work, I should talk to Mr Hacker!

I had no intention of telling Bob and left it at that; and, to be fair, she did improve – somewhat frostily. At surgery the following evening she gave me a good deal more factual information on most of the cases.

I was pleased that she had taken note of my comments, but somewhat surprised when, nearing the end of the session, she appeared to be going well over the top.

'Next,' she announced sharply, 'is a scruffy bearded man with a large hat from which protrudes a cock pheasant's tail feather. He has an earring in his right ear and a goat under his arm. They smell! Whether it is the man or the goat or both – I do not know! The goat,' she continued, with a completely stone-faced look, 'is a Nubian, young and in good condition. As to its symptoms, the owner is completely unco-operative and will neither impart any details as to the animal's problem, or indeed his name and address.' Then she gave me one of her special Billings smiles – a mixture of evil contempt and smug satisfaction. 'He wishes to see the Animal Man!'

'Hell hath no fury . . .' I thought.

'Shall I show him in?' she asked.

She was too icy to be 'spoofing', but it all took a bit of believing. So, rather bemused, and wondering what on earth I was about to receive, I just nodded.

'Yes, please, Miss Billings,' I murmured weakly.' Show him in.'

She was absolutely accurate about the smell!

Fortunately, such was its pervasivness that it preceded the odd couple by several yards, giving me enough time to sling some disinfectant onto the examination table and swab it about generously to combat the odorous invasion.

'You the Animal Man?'

The part-generator of the aroma, for, with my instinctive diagnostic powers, I readily perceived the emission to be a joint affair, stood before me.

I nodded in recognition of what was, after all, a basic description of my professional calling.

'My goat! He's sick, man! Real sick!'

Together, they advanced upon my table, the owner shuffling noisily in open-toed sandals, just visible beneath the voluminous baggy cord trousers, suspended precariously from his rotund paunch.

Lifting the goat, which had remained uncannily passive, from beneath the arm of his much tasselled though tattered suede jacket, he placed it gently upon the table.

'This is Inspiration!' he announced.

Then, raising the goat's narrow chin, he directed its gaze towards his face, giving a low whistle as he did so, and added 'I write songs that make young girls cry, an' I sings 'em to my goat. If he likes 'em, I uses 'em. If he doesn't – I don't!' He looked straight at me, his eyes very far away. 'Now ain't that just the simplest thing, man, just the simplest thing?'

'How can you tell?' I asked, quite intrigued by the idea.

'It's the way he shakes his head,' he said, stroking the goat's drooping ears. 'I can tell. I got vibrations with this kid!'

A musical goat, I thought. Well, it was different and I commenced my examination.

'He's got "otitis", Mr . . .?' I announced finally.

'They call me Earring,' he said, giving his own head a shake, so that what looked like a little brass bull-ring in the lobe of his right ear, glistened in the surgery light. 'Now give it to me straight, man,' he said, leaning across the table and pushing his ginger beard close to my face. 'Give it to me straight.'

'Inflammation of the inner ear – the left one. There is a

173

little in the right one, too. However, some ointment applied daily and an injection, which I will give now, should help to clear things up in a few days.'

Earring looked pensive: 'Could that be . . . why he holds his head on one side occasionally? Why he shakes his head occasionally?' I nodded. 'Not the music?'

'Not the music,' I confirmed.

'Man, you've destroyed me,' he said mournfully. 'Really destroyed me!'

'I'm sure you can still write good songs,' I said, as I prepared and injected the antibiotic.

'Good songs,' he said thoughtfully. 'You don' think my music could have caused the trouble. Like bad vibes, man?'

'Of course not,' I told him.

'Good tidings, man! Good tidings!' he said, cheerfully shaking my hand. Then both he and Inspiration returned to Reception to settle his bill.

Minutes later, a flushed Miss Billings came into the consulting room.

'You all right?' I asked.

'Yes, thank you,' she replied, primly.

'Did he pay?' I queried.

'Yes,' she said. 'And he said you were the "greatest" and he's going to write a song about you.' Then her blush deepened. 'He also called me "chick" and asked me what I was doing wasting my life in a dump like this.'

Miss Billings was never the same after Earring's visit; she became quite coy and her sense of humour returned to such a degree that I had difficulty following some of her jokes.

The following night, after a busy session she tripped in with a card and said: 'Just six more and you're finished.'

'Six more!' I spluttered.

'Five small boys and a dog,' she quipped. 'I'll send them in.'

They entered like a bunch of frightened rabbits, swarthy, tousle-headed and smelling of woodsmoke, trailing a biscuit-coloured lurcher at the end of a frayed cord, its presence almost confirming they were from the tinkers' camp at Fern Bridge.

They were a comical little group, dressed in such a variety of clothing, that they looked like a walking jumble sale. Their average age was about nine, the lurcher of course, being younger.

'Can yer look at the dog, sir?' asked the tallest, holding the cord.

'What's the trouble?' I asked the young spokesman.

Expertly, he lifted the animal onto the table.

'His feet it is, sir,' he replied. The spindly, arrow-headed lurcher pointed his nose towards his front paws, as if to emphasise the area in question.

Like all dogs of the greyhound breed, the legs were long and fine – a perfect combination of levers and pulleys that gave their type such speed and grace.

'What's his name?' I asked.

'Spider,' said the smallest of the lads.

The trouble was fairly obvious. Spider's toe joints were enlarged and when I pressed them gently, he withdrew his paw.

'Going lame, is he?' I enquired.

The spokesman nodded. I looked at my clients' motley assortment of footwear – old sandals, shabby daps, wellies and two pairs of boots.

'If your shoes were two feet long, how do you think you'd manage to walk?' I asked.

They looked at me curiously, then at each other.

I lifted up Spider's paws and pointed to his overgrown toenails. I explained that with such long fine leg bones, the condition of the nails would not allow the pads to go squarely on the ground and, as a result, the toe-joints were inflamed.

As I trimmed Spider's nails, they studied my actions as closely as if I had been performing intricate brain surgery. I then advised them to put some cod liver oil in the diet and not to let them grow so long in future.

Shortly after they left the consulting room, Miss Billings returned to say they had no money.

'Don't charge them,' I said. 'They appreciated what I did – put it down to education in pet care.'

She made no comment and, after tidying up, I went into the front office to check the records, just as she was leaving.

'Nice little lads,' I said, coming to Spider's card. 'Did they say thank you?'

'No they didn't,' she replied tartly. 'But I did hear the little one ask why anyone would have boots two feet long?'

'I expect you thought that odd,' I said, about to tell her about what I thought had been rather a good way of explaining things.

'Yes,' she said 'And so did they. The one with the dog said that nobody with any sense would have boots like that and that you must be the daftest vet around!'

And with that, she swept out into the night, slamming the door behind her.

I stood alone in the outer office, surrounded by bottles, ledgers, instruments and pills, and contemplated her words.

\* \* \*

How quickly those early days seemed to pass: before I realised it, five happy years had streamed by and my life had been full and unbelievably pleasurable, in a way I could scarcely have imagined.

The seven-year itch in marriage is well known, but though we were only half-way there, it did not appear that it was going to worry us, for Diana and I were very happy. Sara was now two years old and a great joy to us both; we had also acquired a puppy of Jack Russell origin that we called Branston and, together with a long-haired ginger cat called Tarquin, he made up our little family.

But there is such a thing as a five-year itch in veterinary practice, and though I appeared outwardly content, surprisingly enough it was beginning to affect me. I became decidedly unsettled and although still happy with the day-to-day routine, I was losing the peace of mind that previously I had always taken for granted.

Maybe the cattle exports had something to do with it, for since the Finnish trip I had been to Sweden, Denmark and Holland.

I talked it over with Diana on several occasions. She was more than content, but tried to understand my feelings and concern that although the living was good, the work interesting and rewarding, I was developing doubts as to whether I wanted to spend the next forty years of my life existing in the same pattern.

It was possible that this underlying uncertainty about my future had precluded me from asking Bob Hacker for a partnership. After three or four years in practice, several of my pals who had qualified at the same time, had been offered permanency in their respective practices.

It was quite a boost to the ego to have one's name added to the notepaper, indicating to all and sundry that one had achieved equal status with experienced veterinarians and was no longer in the 'apprentice' class.

Of course, becoming a partner was not just a matter of being offered a share in the business – one had to pay for it as well!

Now, although this was accepted practice throughout the profession, I was not too attracted by the principle. Five years at university and five years hard work helping to keep the business going, seemed quite enough as far as I was concerned, without having to cough up a few thousand pounds for the privilege of continuing to do so for the rest of one's life.

Drugs, equipment and even cars were a fair purchase, but what was termed 'goodwill' was not, as far as I was concerned, really justifiable. Especially as it was based on the previous three years' profits and therefore the more business one had generated, the more one had to pay!

The senior brigade of veterinary surgeons regarded 'goodwill' as a form of pension, based on the fact that they had worked up the business and it was a reward for the fruits of their labours. Hence it was understandable that they should wish to preserve such a tradition.

I well remember old Oswald Brettner, who ran the only other practice in Ledingford, nearly succumbing to apoplexy when I voiced my opinion that I did not believe in the 'goodwill' transaction. At the time, he was trying to sell a major portion of his business to a rather green assistant who was going to have to go heavily into debt in order to purchase.

Brettner went quite purple, called me a 'reactionary', said I had no sense of value and that all Welshman were robbers anyway!

Maybe my attitude had resulted from a combination of a Welsh upbringing and a Scottish education, but apart from my personal feelings, there were Diana and Sara to consider; if I was going to make any major alterations to my situation, I realised that they should not be left too long.

It was summertime on Bradnor Hill when, one Saturday afternoon, we drove as far up the slopes as possible, then left the car and the four of us, Di, Sara, Branston and myself, walked over the tightly-knit, grassy moorland to the summit.

Sara had chased ahead after the puppy, the sky was high and larks, quite out of sight, were joyfully twittering overhead. Below and all around a heat haze misted the fields and hedgerows, and wooded valleys lost themselves in the distance before the land grew into hills; the Malverns in the east, the Clee to the north and the Black Mountain rounding off the Borders to the south.

A child's laughter, a puppy's bark, a loving wife, the peace and beauty of rural England all around – suddenly I knew that this was for me and here was where I wanted to stay.

As I looked across the gentle, rolling countryside I made my choice.

'I'm going to ask Bob Hacker for a partnership,' I said.

Di turned, her face alight with happiness. She put her

arms around me. 'Oh, darling!' she said. 'That's wonderful, but are you sure?'

'Absolutely,' I said, pulling her close. 'This is for us.'

The following Monday morning I asked Bob Hacker for a share in the firm and a permanent position.

He refused.

True, not as bluntly as that, but he said he did not feel the business could stand three partners. He had to take into account that there could be a down-turn in agricultural prosperity, a factor that was always a possibility.

In the event of 'hard times', room had to be left for contraction, a reduction if necessary to a two-man practice, not three – and if that should occur, the expendable man would have to be the assistant.

I could see the logic, but never had I considered that work would fall off; in fact, since I had been in Ledingford I was sure business had increased – I knew it had. Much of it I had generated myself. There was the Sheep Scheme, the Dairy Clinics – surely those two innovations in themselves justified my asking.

Bob admitted that things were more buoyant than before I had arrived, but, somewhere along the line, he was not over-optimistic about the future.

'Not to say that we couldn't consider it some time,' he said, 'and I'll certainly keep it constantly in mind. But just not at the moment, Hugh. Sorry!'

I drove home to Putsley, numbed at his reaction, utterly disillusioned and completely toppled from my pedestal of complacency.

To my surprise and indeed to my wonderment, Diana took the news without any untoward emotion. Her reaction was one of complete understanding and sympathy for me – she knew how deflated I felt.

'Not the end of the world, darling,' she comforted.

But for me, if not the end, it was an abrupt collision with the vagaries of life, such that I had never experienced before. For the next few weeks, my heart just went out of the job. I even envied old Brettner's assistant, now his partner, despite all my 'reactionary' feelings prior to my rejection.

So many thoughts were constantly on my mind – emigration. New Zealand was a possibility. Several of my pals had settled there or in Tasmania. Then I deliberated on putting up my 'plate' – going it alone – though not within thirty miles of Ledingford: I was prevented from doing that by agreement.

I was in limbo and, for the first time that I could remember, desperately unhappy.

Crossroads had often presented themselves in my life and, so far, I had to admit, the route I had taken had always led to good fortune. Now I had reached another crossroads, but the choice of routes seemed clouded; in fact, I did not appear to have any choice at all.

What was going to be my next move?

It came in the form of a phone call – from Ernie Shelton.

Had I, at that time, been asked to come up with something that could raise my spirits, I know I would never in a million years have thought of anything remotely associated with what he had to say. Even to this day, if I repeat it to myself, it gives me a thrill.

'Hugh!' said Ernie. 'I want you to go to China!'

# 12

Over the following weeks, my unsettled attitude towards my career evaporated rapidly as I concentrated on the epic journey ahead – six thousand five hundred miles across the face of the world to Red China, with fifty Hereford bulls.

There were no quarantine requirements prior to transit as in other shipments and all the preliminary tests were done by the owners' veterinary surgeons at their farms, initial selection having been made by a purchasing team delegated by the Hereford Society.

There were twelve bulls going from our own practice and it was felt prudent that McBean should test these, to avoid any suggestion of bias on my part, for, odd as it seemed, as transit vet, apart from the Ministry of Agriculture, I had ultimate authority as to which animals travelled.

I remember Mac suggesting this in the office at St Mark's Square one afternoon, in front of Bob.

'Hugh's the Big White Chief on this one,' he said. 'Probably get the OBE for services to export!'

I was about to suggest that a partnership would do, but I just looked at Bob and did not pursue it. After all, for me it was a unique opportunity and the fact that I had been asked specifically to do the job, even though still an assistant, was in itself, a pretty good boost.

Diana was equally thrilled.

'You'd better call in at Mr Wang's and get some tips on chopsticks!' she said – a joke at the time, but something that would certainly have benefited me at a later date!

'September the 2nd, from Gatwick,' announced Ernie,

'subject to them all satisfying the physiological tests, quality and consanguinity requirements – and all looking like that . . .' He dropped a Society brochure on the desk in front of me, opened at pages eight and nine.

On the left-hand side were two photographs of a Hereford bull, one taken from the side and the other from behind. Eighteen areas, signified by arrows leading to numbered boxes, were explained in the 'key' on the opposite page. For example:

| | | |
|---|---|---|
| 2 | HEAD | White. Forehead broad, short from muzzle to eye. |
| 8 | BACK | Broad with level topline throughout. Loins wide and well covered with flesh. |
| 10 | QUARTERS | Wide, deep and well filled out, well let down between hind legs. |
| 17 | FETLOCK | Strong. Feet well shaped and adequate to carry the great weight of the animal. |

And finally:

The animal should have a white head and a white crest, white dewlap and throat and white underside, white socks and white brush to the tail. The rest should be a deep red colour.

I studied it and then looked up. 'The perfect bull,' I said.

'Correct!' Ernie, puffing intensely at his great pipe, stood at the window, his back towards me, surveying the jumbled rooftops of Ledingford. 'Correct,' he repeated, 'and that is where we could be in trouble.'

'Trouble!' I said. 'Already?'

He turned slowly to face me. 'Thing is,' he explained, 'we are supplying and transporting; we didn't actually do the deal, that was left to the Export Company. They just gave me the specifications of age and family relationship, the consanguinity as they say – and that's a new one on me. Did you know . . .' he pointed the stem of his pipe directly at me, 'that one request is that "no kindred relations are to exist between the bulls for three generations"? That is not easy!'

'But you've done it,' I said, not quite understanding his concern. 'And the veterinary tests are pretty standard – I've seen them. So where's the trouble?'

'The trouble, my boy, lies in that photograph!'

I shook my head, mystified.

Ernie continued. 'I didn't know until this morning that those photographs were attached to the agreement – which was accepted – asking for fifty bulls as shown in the picture.'

'O, come off it, Ernie!' I said. 'Don't tell me that if they don't all look exactly like that specimen, the Chinese won't accept them!'

'There's an old Chinese proverb,' said Ernie. 'In the market place, everything is equal.'

'And only bachelors' wives and old maids' children are perfect,' I countered.

'You mark my words,' he persisted. 'I've dealt with these oriental boyos before.'

'So, what do I do – bring 'em back?'

Ernie smiled. 'No, Hugh. It won't come to that, they want them too badly; but I'll bet when it comes to paying, there's going to be some pretty inscrutable arguments!'

However, the financial arrangements were not my responsibility, neither was the breed type selection; my job was to ensure that, of the fifty bulls that left the Borders, all fifty would arrive fit and healthy at Shanghai.


I travelled down to Gatwick with Bryn Thomas, in his stock lorry. Diana had taken me to Sonning Court where he was picking up a bull belonging to Tom Brightwell.

It was a strange moment, stepping up into that cab – my last foot on Herefordshire soil before China; maybe I was making more of the situation than it really justified, but I can remember that incident so clearly. Odd moments such as that often stick very firmly in the memory. It is not just that they can be factually recalled, but they tend to come back accompanied with the sounds, smells and even colours of the happening.

It was late summer and already some of the leaves on the tall sycamores that rimmed the farm were turning yellow. The morning was damp and the yard full of irregularly shaped puddles; dampness in the countryside seems to enhance the very essence of life in the plants, hedgerows and grasses, as an earthy, vital aroma fills the air.

Whether, because of the scale of my journey, I was more aware of leaving my roots, I don't know, but suddenly I felt very much attached to the surroundings and realised again how much it all meant to me.

In the barns, the cattle were lowing and moving about, their activity sparked off by the presence of the strange lorry – for to them, lorries are associated with disturbance and often separation; not all journeys are so extended and adventurous as this one. Some, by unfortunate contrast, are short and very final.

One could even believe the excitement of the moment had affected them, as they stretched their heads and craned their necks to get a glimpse of the departure, happy, perhaps, in the thought that one of their company had been selected for such a unique honour.

As we drove out of the yard, I waved back to Di.

It had been a brief and rather formal parting, with Bryn, Tom Brightwell and his men all standing about – just a quick kiss and a hug. I knew I should have made more of it. Damn! On the way to China and already got it wrong! Anyway, I could ring her from Gatwick – that would put things right.

'The wife goin' to miss you,' observed Bryn, as he heaved the great lorry onto the main road.

'Don't know about that,' I said, wondering how he had managed to guess my thoughts.

'Won't be away long, though, will yer?'

In fact, come to think of it, I would not. For nobody had

been granted any visas to stay in China and I was to return on the same plane.

'About six days,' I said.

Bryn grunted and pulled back the stick into top gear. ''Ardly worth goin' all that way just for six days. Christ! I goes to Bognor for longer than that!'

It was an odd comparison, but somehow it did put things in perspective; so instead of feeling like Marco Polo, I told myself I was Hugh Lasgarn doing nothing really extraordinary, threw my sentimental feelings out of the window and settled down to enjoy the trip.

★ ★ ★

On the first leg, we had been airborne for about three hours when the First Officer, an Australian named Doug Kent, came down for a break from the flight deck of the British Caledonian Boeing 707.

He was very interested in the cattle, his folks being farmers themselves. I, of course, was equally interested in the flight and the position of the aircraft.

'About where are we now?' I enquired, as Doug leaned over the crate to rub the curly forehead of one of the Haven bulls.

He turned his wrist and gave a casual glance at his watch.

'Waal,' he said, in his Antipodean drawl, 'we're just abaart flyin' down over South Eastern Europe, an' I'll bet this is the biggest load of bull they've had over Turkey for a long time!'

It was certainly the biggest load of bull I had ever been cooped up with.

We had left the Charlwood lairage, just a few miles from Gatwick where the bulls had been assembled, at two o'clock that morning. Then we had trucked our travellers to the airport loading bay, after I had completed my final examinations and ensured that all the numbers and certificates tallied.

At Gatwick, there was a hold-up due to an impending

strike by the loaders – it was cold, drizzling and dark. Not a very auspicious start to a great adventure.

Following some rapid negotiations between the agent and the disgruntled workers, with quite a few 'greenbacks' exchanging hands to facilitate an agreement, we commenced loading.

Each lorry in turn was backed up and the bulls led into large metal crates, four bulls to a crate. The top was netted, then the whole package raised on a scissors lift to the level of the cargo door of the Boeing, where it was rolled inside to slot onto rails that ran the length of the fuselage. Each crate locked against its neighbour, the end result resembling a series of railway trucks, thirteen in all, accommodating over thirty tons of snorting, steaming muscle and blood.

By 04.30 hours loading was completed and, by 05.15, we lifted off for China.

There were four take-offs and four landing stages during the flight – with a flying time of nineteen and a half hours and a total transit time of twenty-three hours, refuelling at Bahrain, Bangkok and Hong Kong.

At Bahrain, the heat was quite unbelievable, especially after the cold, grey dawn we had left at Gatwick, and I paid ten shillings for a pint of Whitbread in the airport bar – an act that would have broken McBean's heart.

During take-off and in flight, the behaviour pattern of the cattle produced a few problems. Some bulls lay back upon their halters and, with lack of space to obtain sufficient momentum to rise, got into awkward positions. With just a foot-wide gangway up the port side and the only access to the crates over the top, sorting them out was not without physical stress. The poor quality of some of the halters produced knots that were difficult to release, and I resolved to develop a better system when I returned home, one that was more flexible and easier to release.

Next stop was Bangkok, where we were greeted by a chorus of bull-frogs and the dry heat of the Gulf was exchanged for a sticky humidity. While stretching my legs,

I was suddenly surrounded by three armed guards, menacingly pointing their automatics, and was briskly escorted back to the plane.

Doug Kent laconically summed up the incident: 'Hugh, mate! With these guys it's "shoot first – questions after". You're a bloody sight safer in with your bulls than walking around this goddam place!'

Thankfully, it was not long before we were up and away to Hong Kong with our beefy cargo.

As 'veterinary steward', I only offered drinks on landing, but hay was available during flight and nibbled occasionally, as one might take a light snack on a tourist flight – but, unlike some human counterparts, there was no excess consumption, and the duty-free allowance was of no concern to my passengers whatsoever!

However, as far as other comforts went, there the similarity ended, for the interior of the plane was completely devoid of luxuries. No soft music, internal cladding or decoration, the lining was bare to the skin – and this was responsible for another unexpected discomfort.

Cabin temperature was controlled to some extent by electric fans on top of the crates and ran at about 60°F, but all the moisture in the air, such as that exhaled by the bulls – and with fifty pairs of heaving lungs, there was quite a bit of it – adhered to the fuselage roof as a frozen skin. This meant that on dropping from our flight path of 37,000 feet for an approach to land, the temperature rose and the film of ice melted almost immediately, so that it virtually rained inside the plane.

The first time it happened, everything and everybody got soaked; however, once grounded, we were immediately hooked up to a land-based, refrigerated turbo-ventilator and dried out in no time. But soaking, drying, sweating and sleeping in the same clothes was not very comfortable – and I know Diana would have gone mad if she had known!

Coming into Kai-Tak, the precarious landing strip at Hong Kong, I was up on the flight deck.

So far during the trip we had needed three changes of crew, each and every one of them most congenial, but Captain Hillard, who was flying us in at that point, was indeed the most phlegmatic of the pilots.

'There are two approaches to this island,' he explained, as he dipped the nose for the final run-in. 'One is difficult and the other, bloody difficult – we're on the second one!'

I remember commenting that the landing area appeared to be at right angles to our flight path.

'Quite true,' he said, drumming his fingers on his knee. 'See those flats ahead?' He nodded forward to some very tall buildings straight ahead. 'The Honkers living there are always looking out of the windows, so down we go until we see the whites of their eyes – and then it's "left hand down hard"!'

I was quite relieved when we landed.

It had been dark in Bangkok and was dark back in Ledingford, for my time clock registered two in the morning, but in Hong Kong it was breakfast time, bright, sunny and a hive of activity. However, after a welcome wash and a change of clothes, I did not miss the lost hours at all.

We took on a Chinese radio officer and navigator, both dressed simply in slacks and short-sleeved shirts, with an array of pens in their breast pockets. In comparison with the very smartly attired B-Cal crew, they appeared quite boyish, but without them, we were not allowed to fly Chinese airspace. Despite their simple appearance, I later learned that the same two young gentlemen had navigated President Nixon's plane on his visit to China – some contrast in cargo!

We landed in Shanghai at mid-day, Chinese time, and I shall never forget the sight as we rolled down the runway. It seemed as if the whole of Red China was there to greet us – thousands ringing the tarmac, all wearing their party outfits of high-neck blue denim jackets and trousers, and, as the engine noise died away, the chanting of Maoist slogans reached my ears.

Everybody was smiling – I had never seen such outwardly happy people – and all the impressions I had developed of Red China seemed questionable. Yet there did seem to be an uncanny uniformity, apart from the obvious one of dress: a certain stereotyping of 'body language'.

'They are all from the communes to which your bulls are going,' the Chinese radio operator informed me. 'They are joyful you have come.'

Most certainly they looked it. What a contrast to Gatwick's cold, miserable weather and cold, miserable people – maybe I was influenced by the novelty of it all, maybe I was being naïve in my interpretation. But they say first impressions hold more than half of the truth, and those were mine of Communist China, albeit through the porthole of a rather sophisticated cattle transporter.

A delegation of about thirty matching Chinese were waiting at the foot of the gangway.

There was much handshaking, nodding, smiling, bowing and calls of 'Welcome'. Several interpreters chatted amongst the gathering and it was suggested that we should have refreshments and 'much talk'.

When I asked if they would like to inspect the bulls, I was very courteously informed that in no way would they insult my integrity by doubting the correctness of the consignment.

However, remembering Ernie's misgivings as to the matching of the cattle, I felt it was important that I should see the purchasers' reactions, so, through the interpreter, I played a little of their own game by intimating that I would be most offended if I did not have the opportunity of introducing the bulls to them personally.

The idea tickled their fancies and a good section of the delegation squeezed up the plane behind me for a preliminary view. To my relief, no adverse comments were made and they all nodded and made complimentary noises, or at least they sounded so.

In view of the ground temperature, which was well in the 90s, I was keen for the bulls to be off-loaded as soon as

possible, but could see no signs of any official airport hand-
lers – everyone appeared the same!

'They will be taken soon,' said the interpreter in answer
to my enquiry. Yet how that was to be done I could not
fathom, for there was no sign of a scissors lift as was used
at Gatwick, essential for lowering the crates to the ground
before the bulls could be released.

'Seem a bit short on equipment,' I said to Doug Kent.

'Machinery is sufficient!' The interpreter intervened
sharply. 'It is not good to over-mechanise; that is bour-
geois – decadent!'

'You still got to get the beef off the plane,' drawled
Doug, 'an' without a lift it's goin' to be bloody hard!'

'Hardship is the Spirit of Revolution!' came the rapt
reply, 'and we are all fighters in the Revolution. Every
fighter must be prepared to give his energy – to sweat!
Sweating expels non-proletarianism from the body! Sweating big sweat is good thing!'

I was quite taken aback by the outburst. The words came
sharply, arrogantly, brooking no riposte. It was idealism,
saturated idealism. And my first impressions were in
doubt.


If I needed any further conversion to the real truth of
Maoist philosophy, it came when the crates started to be
removed.

Along with a motley collection of cattle trucks that
rattled in convoy up to the plane, there also came a lift, but
it was more of a simple ramp than an elevated platform,
and the crates could not be slid from the interior of the
plane because the lip did not fit flush to the fuselage. This
meant that each crate containing four bulls would have to
be lifted over the ridge between plane and ramp, before it
could be lowered to the floor.

There was no means of lifting the crates by pulley or
crane – mechanisation being decadent!

So they lifted them bodily. Hundreds, or seemingly
hundreds, of squawking, chattering, straining, sweating

bodies – they lifted the crates over the hump and lowered them onto the shaky lift, and thence to the floor.

And as they did so, their facial expressions changed from happiness to hardship as they sweated the big sweat – the Spirit of the Revolution!

Only then did I realise, in just a small way, the implications of Maoism to the individual, and could understand when later it became known why the new 'peasant Jerusalem' was a futile dream, destined for failure and disillusionment – a doomed experiment in the annals of dictatorship.

Whether the spectacle was felt to be an embarrassment and not to be dwelt upon by Western eyes, I do not know. For I was not allowed to stay overlong, the interpreter taking me by the arm and leading me away, saying we should go for refreshments and the 'much talk'.

It was impossible to refuse and I left them to it, wondering indeed, what the Herefords were going to think of it all!


The conference was held in the airport building, in a large room which contained a single gigantic table in the shadow of a massive statue of Chairman Mao himself, placed in such a position that, wherever one sat, his all-seeing eyes could be felt, burning into one's neck.

There was a rather ritualistic atmosphere about the proceedings, like being in a temple talking to the disciples, with communion being celebrated, not with wine and incense, but with tea and cigarettes!

The tea was clear and green, served in tall china mugs, and the infusion topped up with hot water from thermos flasks, which seemed most odd. Despite the distance I had travelled and the fact that it really was authentic China tea, I still could give it no other description than when I had first tasted it back home – that of 'gipsy's shaving water'!

As for the cigarettes, the Chinese smoked enormous numbers and the air soon became blue and heavily scented; as I sat there in the midst of the oriental gathering and surveyed the assembled company, boyhood memories of Charlie Chan and Fu Manchu trickled through my mind – this was certainly a long way from the Capitol Cinema in Abergranog!

Then we launched into the 'much talk', which took off on a rather different tack from that which I had anticipated.

As well as Ernie's exhortations to ensure that all the documentation was in order, I had also had a briefing from the Society Committee. They were most concerned that the Chinese should be given the fullest information about the Hereford breed, in the hope that this consignment would be just the first of more to come. As a result, I had spent many nights doing my homework prior to the trip and was now prepared to answer the most intricate questions in the minutest detail; anything from haematological values to conversion ratios and fertility regimes.

The first question I was asked was: 'How long does bull live?'

It was such a devilishly simplistic question, that I was stuck for an immediate answer!

Maybe it was the effect of 'jet-lag' creeping in, something to which I assumed the bulls were immune. I had heard it said that the disorientation caused by travelling across the time band did odd things to the brain, and in my case it was manifesting itself in my inability to deliver such an obvious fact.

It was a bit like 'how long is a piece of string?'

'It all depends', is the reasonable way to tackle it, but then, I could sense they were looking for a positive response and I was proved correct when, after giving what I considered to be an acceptable range, the interpreter asked if I could be more precise!

There followed questions of equally straightforward content.

'How much water does bull drink?'

'How much hay does bull eat?'

To these queries, I answered with exact amounts, after again being requested to be more precise.

It was a most odd discussion and the Chinese appeared to be writing down every word I uttered. As they did so. I wondered how much my integrity, which they were so keen to honour, would be damaged if one of the bulls should not survive to the declared age or should drink an extra bucket of water.

I fervently hoped all the Herefords would pull together, do the decent thing and match up to my figures!

I did get an opportunity, eventually, to mention some other factors, such as the metabolic diseases and mineral deficiencies, and provided as much information about them as I could.

They all listened courteously, nodding as I spoke to my words translated through the interpreter, whose musical tone as he babbled on made my description of hypomagnesaemia and hepatitis sound like a joyfully funny story.

The meeting lasted about an hour and then, together with the aircrew, I was taken on a motor tour of Shanghai – another unforgettable experience.

As we drove along, shades of the Capital Cinema in Abergranog again passed before me, for that was where I first became acquainted with Shanghai – the Opium Den of the East. Supplied by the Western traders, Britons among them, and the 'White Death' traded with the wretched addicts for silver and jade.

To be 'Shanghaied' – 'Arrh, lad! Now there be a story!'

Then the missionary dying a terrible death, uttering his last croaking words: 'If God endures Shanghai, He owes an apology to Sodom and Gomorrah!'

How Wendel Weekes and I shivered in the cheap seats of the 'flea-pit' on Saturday afternoons, the very word 'Shanghai' bringing pimples to our butties.

And here I was, right amongst it!

'Oh Wendel, boyo! 'Ew should 'ave seen it!'

Actually, despite the colourful hell that I had imagined in my boyhood days, the scene was comparatively innocuous.

There were eleven million people living in Shanghai and on the afternoon we drove, or rather threaded, through, they all seemed to be there – half of them riding bicycles!

On the waterfront it was the same, with a variety of craft defying description.

Apart from normal cargo boats, the traditional sailing craft, with their triangular lateen sails, wove in and out of strings of lighters, seven and eight long, towed by low barges. The whole scene was accompanied, unbelievably, with more hooting and pandemonium than in the streets – chaotic rather than sinister. Our guide was pointing out various important features and landmarks, but for me, the buildings and monuments took second place to the ferment of humanity all around.

Finally, we arrived at a rather plain edifice, where we assembled in a large hall and were subsequently entertained to a 'real' Chinese meal.

What a welcome sight it was, for I was starving.

We were seated round a circular table, one of the Chinese group alternating with one of ours.

The centre had a revolving section laden with exotic delights that made the eyes pop, and all the more mouthwatering after the snack meals provided in-flight.

There was fish of all descriptions, glazed duck, fruits, savouries, delicate rolls and pork in all manner of guises, countless dishes I could not even begin to recognise – and there were chopsticks!

Diana's suggestion that I should have approached Mr Wang for lessons suddenly came home to me. All these delights and me with an appetite to match – and two knitting pins to eat with.

As the centre-piece slowly revolved, our Chinese hosts selected various pieces which they presented to us and, as even picking up anything at arm's length with the equipment provided was a feat in itself, I was content to be supplied by my neighbour.

Tackling the food from the plate was not as impossible as I had anticipated and I found that by selecting small portions and keeping my head fairly low down, I could bridge the gap reasonably well.

I was even feeling rather pleased with my progress, especially when my host said: 'You use chopstick very well!' But I was more than a little bemused when he added: 'Ah! you have hand like lady!'

I never quite fathomed that one and perhaps it was just as well!

Neither did I ever know if Doug Kent was serious when he said how much he had enjoyed the meal, never having had Bear's Paw, Camel Hump, Sea Slug and Elephant's Nose in Soy Sauce before!

Maybe I should have examined some of the delights more closely, but by then it was far too late.

I did not see the bulls again, either, for during the entertainment and discussions they had been spirited away. When we arrived back at the airport, the Boeing was cleaned out and ready to leave.

Such was the perpetual motion of the whole trip that I did not feel any unusual sentiment as we took off, for my mind was in a state of gentle confusion, eased by a few hours' sleep which I snatched on the way back to Hong Kong.

A hurricane formed from a tropical depression in the South China Sea grounded us at Kai-Tak for three days – an ill wind that blew a bit of good for me, because I was able to take a look at the Colony in between gusts and make some purchases for home.

I bought Diana a silk dress, some shoes for Sara and had a suit for myself made in a day, something my wife found nearly impossible to believe; not just the speed of the work, but the fact that I had bought it at all.

'I can't even get you to buy a pair of socks in Ledingford,' she ribbed, on my return. 'But send you to the other side of the world and you buy all this!'

In fact, it was a good suit and the material first quality.

On the return flight, the Boeing carried jeans for the United Kingdom.

They were packed in massive bundles and covered in sacking – a very different cargo, quieter, less demanding, completely independent of any veterinary attention and the ideal form of palliasse, for which I was truly grateful.

To say that I took advantage of the relative comfort would be an understatement – and I have a certificate to prove it, embossed with a photograph of the plane and signed by all the crew. It reads: 'To Hugh Lasgarn, Long Distance Vet – The Only Man to Sleep 25 Hours On A 20-Hour Flight!'

That was the trip to China – just six days – but the time, though short, so full of rich experience and so essential by its contrast in enhancing my affection for the Borders.

And an integral part of that experience had to be the Herefords. What grand ambassadors they were for us – no language barriers, political hang-ups, religious differences. Wherever they went, they represented us so honestly and I was proud to be associated with them. Without them I would have missed out on so much, bringing home again to me the degree to which animals had entered into my life.

Not just my life, either, but everybody's, even transcending race barriers. This was poignantly summed up after the reception in Shanghai, during a round of speeches which followed the banquet. I had been requested to say a few words, and the reply to my toast was given by an old, wizened Chinese gentleman.

He raised his tiny glass with a shaky hand and, through the interpreter, said:

> 'You are our guests and we honour you.
> You are our friends and we respect you.
> You are our brothers and we love you.'

Sentiments that were manifested simply through the presence of a bunch of bulls and a vet from the Welsh Borders.

And what of Ernie's cynical suggestion that they would quibble over the fact that the cattle did not match – well, brotherly love only stretches so far in business and Ernie was 'correct'! In fact, I do not think the full price was ever paid; but, looking back, if anyone got value for money from that China export, it was Hugh Lasgarn!

\* \* \*

There followed fairly rapidly on the tail of my China visit, two exports to Sweden and one to Spain where, in the heat of the Iberian sun, I experienced my first 'corrida'.

We had shipped the consignment from Newpool to Pasajes on the Basque coast and trucked the cattle down to Valdepenas, south of Madrid.

I stayed on for a few days with Señor Arturo Gomez and his charming wife on their estancia in the Guadiana valley. He was a highly respected and very influential man and had developed his vast acres along the river, cultivating and irrigating until, even in high summer, the pasture land resembled, quite closely, the watermeadows of the River Wye.

In fact, such was the similarity that I knew the cattle would be happy there.

In my honour they gave a party, a grand affair with a gigantic barbeque, dancing and much wine. It was a fantastic evening, my only regret being that Diana was not there to enjoy it with me.

As the festivity drew to a close, I sought out the Señor to thank him for his hospitality.

'It is my pleasure!' he proclaimed expansively. 'And tomorrow, my good friend, I take you to the bullfight!' He slapped me heartily across the shoulders. 'You will enjoy it!'

I thanked him for the invitation, but as for enjoying it – that was a different matter.

Señor Gomez turned away to bid farewell to some other guests; as he did so, his wife took me to one side.

The Señora Gomez was a beautiful woman, tall, dark and of elegant bearing.

'Hugh,' she said. 'I think it is not for you, the bullfight.'

'Why do you say so?' I asked.

'You have different feelings for your animals than those who love the bullfight,' she said softly. I shook my head slightly and smiled with mild embarrassment. 'I know,' she continued. 'I know when you look at our land and say your bulls will be happy here, and I see how you care for them and respect them.'

I thanked her for her concern. 'But I *should* see it,' I replied. 'I should at least experience it.' It was her turn to shake her head, gently and sadly.

'What will you think of us?' she said.

'I suppose your countrymen also have a respect for their bulls, but more for their aggression, and I have heard it said that the bullfight is a ballet of death and glory, even though the die is cast before it has begun.'

She nodded. 'Yes, for the true matador, that is so. It is for him honour, skill and bravery, but there are many cheats – and that is not good.'

The cheats, I was later to learn, were the fights involving 'half-bulls', ones overfed, unfit and of low fighting ability, that made the matador look falsely brave; or the shaved horns, so tender that the bull was reluctant to charge; or the lances doctored so that they could pierce further than the 'rules' permitted.

I went to the bullfight and I was sickened.

Señor Gomez admitted that it was not a good one – only one bull was killed really cleanly and even that had been reduced to a shambling hulk by the obsessive attention of the 'picadors'. For me, there was little ballet in it and the die very much cast in favour of the matadors – though one did get severely tossed and I found myself inwardly pleased that, in my book, some justice had been done.

What an odd world, I thought, and even an odder turn of mind that I should secretly delight in seeing one of my 'brothers', as the old Chinaman had called us all, coming off second best to a bull.

Yet the crowds went wild at the killing, hungry for blood and excitement; they roared, cheered, whistled, blew trumpets, banged drums. And all to celebrate the death of a bull.

'A vet who enjoys killing for pleasure is like an upholsterer who slashes furniture for fun!' So said Oswald Brettner, the old vet whom I first met at a point-to-point, and how right he was. They say that if one can see the bullfight and last for a year without seeing another, then one is not an 'afficionado'. I have never seen one since – and many years have passed.

Still, it was wonderful to be a transit vet and see the world, and wherever I went on the 'tail' of the Herefords, I returned home richer for the experience.

The religious constraints in Morocco, the poverty in Brazil, the racial tension in Africa, each trip moulding my outlook to a degree I could scarcely have credited, when first I went to Ledingford. I could feel my personality altering, changing from being introspective and parochial, developing a greater and far more realistic awareness.

I was beginning to realise that, although bulls and budgerigars were 'beings' and my life was set to care for them and respect their place in the earthly pattern, my fellow humans, too, were equally in need of care and consideration, and not just within the shadow of the Black Mountain and the Wye Valley.

# 13

Racialism, communism, cultural modes – these are factors not uppermost in the rural scene. Yet the Borders were no strangers to religious and political wrangles over the years. Saxon, Celt, Norman and Roman all vigorously asserted their points of view from time to time, the legacies of their 'feuding an' a'fightin'' enduring in the castles, battlefields, churches and earthworks.

Hard to appreciate, when one stood on the high ground of Ladylift on the north side of Ledingford, surrounded by natural tranquillity and earthy goodness, that in such places terror and bloodshed could ever have been commonplace. The Battle of Mortimer's Cross, the sacking of Ledingford Cathedral, the Civil War, the marauding Welsh. Suffering by the inhabitants of the Borders fully equalled that of the Chinese peasants, South African blacks, Brazilian poor or the persecuted religious minorities around the world in present times. Yet, after the storm, these were the calm waters and all the angst had passed, dealt with by our warrior forefathers and bequeathed to people like myself.

My travels about the world on the 'tails' of the Herefords had not only opened my eyes to the humanitarian struggles and complexities overseas, but had made me take a closer look at my own good fortune – in living where someone else had sorted things out, long before I was born.

Indeed, after the storm of my own uncertainty, there were calm waters ahead and good fortune smiled on me again, in the shape of McBean's betrothal!

It was an unqualified surprise when he announced that

he and Mimi Lafont, his longstanding yet still vivacious girlfriend, were to be wed.

In full Irish fashion, the wedding was an hilarious affair: McBean's whole family 'crossed the water' for the occasion, to provide the true party spirit.

But the biggest surprise of all came in his wedding speech, when, after thanking everyone from the vicar down to the hotel cat, he announced that Mimi and he would shortly be leaving Ledingford for his homeland, where he had recently inherited a small farm in County Clare, overlooking the Shannon.

There, he said, with the old twinkle in his eye, he would put up his feet, relax and perhaps grow a few Mc'Beans!

\* \* \*

I was to miss my colleague very much, for in my early days he was a wonderful support and gave me boundless encouragement – albeit with a fair touch of the blarney; however, his departure meant Bob Hacker was on his own and it was not long before I was offered a partnership.

After a brief consultation with Di, I took it.

'HACKER & LASGARN M'SRCVS' – at last I had my name on the plate; and even my wanderlust was satisfied as well, for we moved.

But not a great distance. Just twelve miles northwest of Ledingford on the far side of Ladylift, to the lovely old half-timbered village of Welbury – Diana, Sara, Joanna our new daughter, Tarquin the cat and Branston the Jack Russell.

From being a vet in green pastures, I had matured to a vet for all seasons, weathered my personal 'storm' and found my haven in a peaceful and beautiful Herefordshire village.

Vet in a village: what a good title for a book!

# Fontana Paperbacks
# Non-fiction

Fontana is a leading paperback publisher of non-fiction.
Below are some recent titles.

Armchair Golf *Ronnie Corbett* £3.50
You Are Here *Kevin Woodcock* £3.50
Squash Balls *Barry Waters* £3.50
Men: An Owner's Manual *Stephanie Brush* £2.50
Impressions of My Life *Mike Yarwood* £2.95
Arlott on Wine *John Arlott* £3.95
Beside Rugby *Bill Beaumont* £3.50
Agoraphobia *Robyn Vines* £3.95
The Serpent and the Rainbow *Wade Davies* £2.95
Alternatives to Drugs *Colin Johnson & Arabella Melville* £4.95
The Learning Organization *Bob Garratt* £3.95
Information and Organizations *Max Boisot* £3.50
Say It One Time For The Broken Hearted *Barney Hoskins*
    £4.95
March or Die *Tony Geraghty* £3.95
Nice Guys Sleep Alone *Bruce Feirstein* £2.95
Royal Hauntings *Joan Forman* £3.50
Going For It *Victor Kiam* £2.95
Sweets *Shona Crawford Poole* £3.95
Waugh on Wine *Auberon Waugh* £3.95

You can buy Fontana paperbacks at your local bookshop or
newsagent. Or you can order them from Fontana Paperbacks,
Cash Sales Department, Box 29, Douglas, Isle of Man. Please
send a cheque, postal or money order (not currency) worth the
purchase price plus 22p per book for postage (maximum postage required is £3).

NAME (Block letters) _____

ADDRESS _____

_____

_____